JOHN WESLEY POWELL
Geologist-Explorer

JOHN WESLEY POWELL

Geologist-Explorer

~~~~~~~~~~~~~~~~~~~~~~~~~~~~~~~~~~~~~

Born: March 24, 1834
Died: September 23, 1902

BY DALE WHITE

JULIAN MESSNER, INC.

NEW YORK

Published by Julian Messner, Inc.
8 West 40th Street, New York 18

Published simultaneously in Canada
by The Copp Clark Publishing Co., Limited

Printed in the United States of America
Library of Congress Catalog Card No. *58-10923*

To

RUTH AND GEORGE GRISWOLD

CONTENTS

CONTENTS

JOHN WESLEY POWELL
Geologist-Explorer

CHAPTER ONE

STONED!

Early one September morning in 1843 a small auburn-haired boy dropped an armload of kindling in the box next to the kitchen stove and asked anxiously, "Can I go now, Mama? The woodbox is full up, and the cows out to pasture."

Mary Powell turned from kneading bread dough and smiled at her nine-year-old son, John Wesley Powell. She could think of a dozen more chores for the lad to do, but she knew Wes couldn't be held back another minute. "On your way," she told him, and meant to add, "Wash at the pump and change into your good trousers and shirt." But Wes had already streaked out the door, skinny brown legs and bare feet racing across the back lot. He vaulted the split-rail fence and disappeared into the oak grove marking the outskirts of Jackson, Ohio, a frontier town a few miles north of the Ohio River.

Wes ran through the sun-dappled trees, whooping at the chickadees overhead. When the path strung out across a rolling meadow, he snapped off plumes of goldenrod, stuck them in his hair, and pretended he was an Indian running down a deer. As he pranced full speed across a shallow brook, the warm water splashed over his patched trousers and sleeveless shirt. Not long after, perspiring and breathless, he paused on the threshold of George Crookham's log-cabin library.

"Come in, boy!" a big man boomed from a throne-sized chair

set midway the length of a table strewn with books and maps.

"Good morning, teacher!" Wes answered as he ran across the room and climbed onto a stool.

The inkwell shook as George Crookham burst into laughter. "Teacher!" he exclaimed. "I don't know how good a teacher I'll be, but if size has anything to do with it, I ought to be a humdinger!" When Crookham laughed, his chins quivered. He claimed to be the biggest farmer in Ohio — "three hundred and fifty pounds on the feed-store scales."

Wes had liked this man from the moment he first saw him five years earlier when the Powell family arrived in Jackson after migrating from New York. Wes' father, the Reverend Joseph Powell, tall, stern, and prematurely gray, purchased a town lot and pasture from the huge, wealthy landowner. When Crookham inquired what he planned to do in Jackson, the Reverend explained that he was determined "to bring the Word of God and the teachings of that great Methodist, John Wesley, to win souls for the Kingdom. Amen!"

"You'll be English or Welsh?" Crookham guessed.

Reverend Powell nodded. "A little of both. My wife and I came to this country from London thirteen years ago. We're pledged to carry the Word to the outlands."

"There's a good many English settling around here," the farmer continued. "You'll feel right at home." Then he bowed to Mrs. Powell and the children. "I see you're a family man, Reverend. How do you plan to make a living? Preaching doesn't bring much on the frontier."

Reverend Powell said he was a tailor by trade, and also planned to farm a few acres. Apparently Crookham approved because he prophesied, "You'll prosper at both. There's plenty of sinners out this way, and no other tailor in southern Ohio. As for farming, the soil is gravelly, but it'll grow anything. You'll make out fine."

The Powell family did prosper in their new location. The Reverend and George Crookham became close friends because they agreed on many things, both being against liquor and slavery.

Since there was no school at Jackson, Mrs. Powell, in addition to her thousandfold housekeeping duties, had to teach her growing family their three R's. When the townspeople provided a school in 1843, there were five Powells on hand opening day: Martha and Mary, now fifteen and thirteen; nine-year-old Wes; seven-year-old Bram; and Lida, five. Only the two infants, Nell and Walter, were left at home.

The teacher graded his new pupils by their ability to write, do sums, spell simple words, and read poetry. Martha and Mary had no difficulty because all the older girls sat together on one bench and didn't care who was smartest. Bram and Lida were put in the primary group. Unfortunately Wes began to have trouble his very first day. Because he was exceptionally bright for his age and could quote entire Gospels from the Bible from memory, the teacher put him ahead of older, bigger boys. They resented having a half-grown "pipsqueak" sitting in first place on their bench. The more questions Wes could answer and they flubbed, the more they hated him.

One day the teacher kept Wes a long time after school for spelling practice. On his way home the big boys waylaid him and lined up across the path.

"Where d'ya think you're goin', Mr. Smarty?" one jeered.

Chin up, Wes looked straight up at his taunter and answered, "Home."

"Home," another sneered in singsong. "Home to that nigger-lovin' Pa of yours? If he don't quit preachin' sermons against folks in Ohio ownin' slaves, my Pa says he's gonna get tarred and feathered!"

The threat didn't frighten Wes. His father and men like George Crookham who talked out against slavery were always being threatened, but that didn't stop them. Wes had heard the issue of slavery discussed many times in his home. He had decided that if his father and Big George were against slaveholding, he was too! He didn't mind hearing his father called a "nigger lover." The epithet was one used commonly on people opposed to keeping the Negroes in bondage. Wes had heard his father preach many times that a good Christian should be proud to be called that.

Wes straightened his bony shoulders and said, " 'Sticks and stones may break my bones, but names can never hurt me.' Let me by!" The sun had disappeared behind the trees, and Wes knew the cows would be bawling at the gate for him to take them to the barn for milking.

"Try 'n git by," one of the bullies challenged and knocked Wes off his feet.

He bounded up, flew at the bigger boy, and ended up in the dirt again with his nose bloodied. He tried again and again. Finally one of the gang said, "Aw, let 'im go. He don't know when to quit."

Wes staggered to his feet, mopped his bleeding mouth with his shirt sleeve, and walked away. He refused to run or let the boys think he was scared. He didn't turn when he heard one yell, "Don't try comin' back to school neither! We ain't havin' no nigger lover on the bench with us!" The next thing Wes knew, he was being pelted with stones, some big enough to hurt badly. Still, he refused to run. After a few moments the bullies gave up and Wes limped home.

Mary Powell, aghast at her son's appearance, tended his hurts. She wanted to put on her bonnet and visit the schoolteacher. Not until then did Wes cry. He would not have his mother fighting his fight!

"You walk between Mary and me going to and from school," Martha suggested. "Those bullies don't dare throw stones at girls."

Wes would have none of that either.

Mrs. Powell pleaded, "You've got to go with the girls. You can't give up school, Wes. You're too bright. I'd keep you home but I've taught you all I can, and you keep asking for more. What am I to do? You've got to get an education somehow."

Although he could hardly see or talk because of the pummeling he had suffered, Wes said stubbornly, "I'm going back to school, and I'm not hiding behind any girls."

"But you'll get hurt more," Mary whimpered. "You might get blinded!"

"Or rocked in the head so hard you won't have any sense left, like that boy who got kicked by a horse," Martha wailed.

Mrs. Powell sank in a chair. "What am I to do?" For a moment she was too discouraged to hold back the tears. If only her husband were home, he would know how to handle the situation. Then she sighed and dried her eyes on a corner of her apron. The Reverend was scarcely ever home. Once he saw that his family had a comfortable house and a big garden for Wes and Bram to tend, he left all the work to his wife and children, so he was free to travel to his outland ministry.

Bram, who couldn't take his eyes off his older brother's face, said, "Mama, why don't you ask Big George? He's our best friend."

Martha and Mary chorused, "Yes! Send for Big George. He always comes when we need help."

Although it was dusk and Bram hated walking through the oak grove alone, he was willing to go to Crookham's farm. He found Big George in his "cabinet," a two-room log-cabin museum and library housing the farmer's extensive library and large collections of Indian relics, shells, rocks, flowers and insects.

Before Bram finished stammering out his story, the older man was on his way to the stable to hitch up the stout mare who pulled his specially built buggy. In no time he was waddling across the Powell kitchen and clucking over Wes' face. With the gentlest touch he pried the swollen lids apart and checked Wes' eyes, then his teeth and the lumps on his head. "The bullies!" he sputtered. "Bad cess to the ignorant lot of them!" He was so upset he plumped down on the edge of the bed, unaware of how Mrs. Powell and the girls held their breath for fear it would collapse under his tremendous weight.

"What shall I do?" Mrs. Powell asked. "Wes won't let me tell the teacher. He won't walk to school with the girls. But he's got to have an education. He's starved for learning. There isn't a book or pamphlet his father brings home that he doesn't try to read."

Big George nodded sympathetically. He knew how bright Wes was, had marveled at his amazing ability to memorize long passages from the Bible. But one thing Crookham often regretted was that Wes was growing up in a household where a narrow-minded, too-stern father demanded that his children read only religious writings. Didn't the Reverend realize that it wasn't enough to teach a boy to be a sponge, to soak up volumes of unrelated facts or high-flown recitations? Many times Crookham had wished he could teach the boy. Here was a great mind in the making, he had decided as he watched Wes grow, a fresh, young, eager intellect that ought to be given many fields to explore.

"What am I fuming about?" Crookham exclaimed so suddenly that everyone jumped. "I know how we can solve the problem, easy as pie. "Wes," he asked earnestly, his fat cheeks lifting as he smiled. "How about letting me be your teacher? I mean, how would you like to come over to my library every weekday and study science and history with me?"

That was why, after his bruises healed, young Wes Powell hurried through his chores on a bright September morning and raced all the way to Big George Crookham's library. He couldn't get there fast enough!

CHAPTER TWO

"MAYBE I'LL BE AN EXPLORER!"

As soon as he was settled on the stool, Wes began to worry. What if Big George asked questions he couldn't answer, and decided maybe Wes wasn't so bright after all? "Shall I recite something?" he asked anxiously.

George Crookham shook his head. "Let's just talk. Dibble-dabble around, I call it. Poke our noses into this and that. Look at maps and books and some of the collections in the museum. Would you like that?"

"Oh yes!" Wes agreed quickly, his anxiety dispelled.

"Later we will discuss what you should read," Crookham continued, talking to the nine-year-old as if he were an adult. "But first I want to show you something." The teacher pulled a map in front of Wes. "This is a map of our country, and we are r-i-g-h-t here." His pudgy finger pointed to a small dot.

Wes' forehead wrinkled. His mother had taught him reading, writing, and arithmetic — but not geography. There had been no maps in the Jackson schoolroom. The dot Mr. Crookham was pointing to looked awfully small. Too small. "Jackson is bigger than that," he protested. "It's got a town square and six streets, with houses on them, and a church and stores and a sawmill. Why isn't the dot larger?"

The size of the dot had no relation to the size of the town, merely its location, the teacher explained. "But it does give you

17

an idea, doesn't it, of how small Jackson is, and of how big the rest of the continent is?"

Wes nodded, though this new knowledge was a little hard to grasp. He had lived in Jackson as long as he could remember, since he was four. Its frame houses and log cabins shaded by friendly oak trees, the neighboring woods, and farms had been all the world he had ever known existed, until this very minute. Of course his mother had told him about living in England; but all that Wes had visualized was that England was "far across the water." Now Mr. Crookham was showing him how vast was the world and expecting him to understand. It was kind of like being told to eat an apple in one gulp, instead of bite by bite, when it would be easier to digest.

He looked at the dot intensely, then a wavering line below it. "What's that?"

"The Ohio River."

Wes blinked. That was the broad Ohio! He laughed. If one skinny line represented the biggest river he had ever seen, then he needn't feel badly because Jackson was identified with a small dot. "Where does the Ohio come from?" he asked earnestly, tracing its course to the east with his finger. Big George showed him where the Ohio was formed at Pittsburgh by the junction of the Allegheny and Monongahela Rivers.

"Where does it go?" He was shown where the Ohio flowed into the mighty Mississippi.

Questions spouted from Wes like birds flushed from a blackberry thicket. "What's this?" he asked, excitement making his voice squeak. His fingers traced the shoreline of Lake Erie. "And these funny marks!" He ran his finger down the hatch marks denoting the formidable granite peaks of the Rocky Mountains.

The morning hours passed swiftly as the nine-year-old learned how big America was, and its relation to the rest of the world.

"Is Lake Erie bigger than the pond where I go fishing?" he wondered aloud.

Big George thought a moment. "Pretend the face of the clock

on the wall is Lake Erie, and this button on my shirt is the pond. Does that help you contrast the two?"

Wes grinned. "Yes!" he almost shouted. This kind of school was fun!

Since he could compare the lines on the map, he had an easier time figuring how much longer the Mississippi and Missouri were than the Ohio. But he could not comprehend how high mountains were, even though Big George showed him a sketch of the Alps. "Golleeee, the highest thing I ever climbed is the sawdust pile at the sawmill," he confessed. "Nobody ever climbs 'way to the top of mountains, does he?"

"Certainly!" Crookham assured him. "In a day or two I'll be introducing you to a real mountain climber!" Then he added, "Now don't try to remember everything I've told you today. We will discuss these things again and again, until you really understand. After all, it's taken me forty years to learn all this that I'm telling you. You can't expect to absorb it all in one day."

Wes relaxed. Mr. Crookham evidently wasn't going to be impatient, like the schoolmaster, or demanding, like his father. He could always learn things easiest when his mother taught him because she was soft-voiced and never upset him. "Tell me a story now," he begged.

"All right." Big George knew that if he told his young pupil about the discovery or settlement of certain places marked on the map that they would be more clearly identified for him. He began by telling Wes, "In 1492, Columbus sailed the ocean blue." After describing the three stout ships and the voyage, he followed with an account of the Pilgrims. "They were explorers too — only they were searching for a new way of life," he pointed out.

"Now let's come closer to home," he suggested and told Wes about the great French explorer, Sieur de La Salle, who was said to have discovered the Ohio River in 1669 or 1670, and who built the *Griffin*, the first boat to sail on Lake Erie.

The schooling even continued during lunch. While Wes went

to the well for a pitcher of drinking water, Big George uncovered a basket of food brought from his house. Unlike most people in southern Ohio, Crookham did not eat his dinner at noon, as was the custom. He didn't want to leave his library, and he claimed a heavy meal made him sleepy during the afternoon. So his wife had packed a "light" lunch of fried chicken, cold ham slices on buttered homemade buns, hard-boiled eggs, pickles, potato salad, raw carrots, oatmeal cookies, and sweet cherries from the Crookham orchard.

Wes gaped openmouthed at the food, until he remembered his manners. No wonder the farmer was huge! Wes nibbled a chicken leg and an egg, never taking his eyes off Mr. Crookham's face as he resumed the storytelling with accounts of how the Spanish priests founded the missions in California; what thirst and hardships were suffered by the first traders to blaze the Santa Fe Trail; and why Congress paid Spain 5,000,000 dollars to acquire Florida and its fine stands of timber. It was mid-afternoon and "time to eat a plum or two" when Crookham told Wes about the opening of the Northwest Territory that had drawn thousands of folks like his parents from the Eastern states across Ohio to the frontier neighboring the Great Lakes.

With his elbows propped on his knees and his fists knotted against his cheeks, Wes listened spellbound. When Big George stopped to eat again — "No sense letting these plums get too ripe" — Wes studied the map. It was beginning to make sense now. He could think of a hundred questions to ask, but held his tongue. He didn't want to be like his little sister Lida, who talked all the time now that she had started school. Finally he said, wanting to touch the area on the map but holding back because his fingers were sticky, "Look, there's hardly any marks in this big space between the Mississippi and the mountains. You haven't told me about the — Co-lum-bia River," he said, squinting to read the script lettering. "Hasn't anybody explored out there?"

"Haven't you ever heard about the Lewis and Clark Expedition?"

Wes shook his head. The only stories he had heard at home were about Jesus and the Apostles and John Wesley, the great Methodist for whom he was named.

"Every boy in America should know about Lewis and Clark," Crookham stated emphatically. "It was not only one of the greatest explorations our country will ever know, but also it's a rousing good story of adventure!" The teacher sat straighter and locked his fingers over his huge stomach. Wes hugged his knees to his chest. Another story!

Crookham described how Captains Meriwether Lewis and William Clark, two young Americans, had led an expedition from 1804 to 1806 up the long stretch of the Missouri to its headwaters in the Rocky Mountains. Wes traced the journey on the map. Because he had read the *Journals* published after the captains' return, Big George was able to describe in considerable detail how the men fought grizzlies, killed elk and buffalo for food and clothing, powwowed with the Indians, and felled huge cedar logs to make canoes for floating down the mighty Columbia River to the Pacific Ocean. "You know, Lewis and Clark went down the Ohio, right past the very spot where your father took you for a ride in a rowboat, when they were on their way to St. Louis to make the final preparations for their great westward journey."

Wes closed his eyes. He pictured himself in a buckskin suit like William Clark's, his hand shading his eyes as he searched for the first glimpse of the snow-topped mountains. Then he imagined he was tall, handsome Meriwether Lewis, sitting in the cedar dugout, arms akimbo, every inch the brave explorer! These thoughts were so glorious that Wes shivered! When he opened his eyes, they were sparkling. "Maybe I'll be an explorer someday!" But his dream clouded over. "I've got to grow up first, and I couldn't leave as long as Mother needed me. She has to have a man around the house because Papa is away so much. But there would be places left for me to explore, wouldn't there?"

Crookham leaned over and patted Wes' unruly auburn hair. "Of course, lad! There is always a frontier of some kind that needs opening up. But maybe you'll decide to be something entirely different after we discuss some new subjects tomorrow. You've plenty of time to plan for your future." With a tremendous heave he raised from his chair. "We've traveled far enough for one day, eh, lad? I've got to have my dinner and prepare a lecture for the older fellows who come to the museum two nights a week to study natural history with me. I'll see you in the morning."

Wes stammered his thanks and retraced the path homeward. Only it was no longer a familiar trail meandering across a creek and a meadow. Wes pretended he was Meriwether Lewis tracking a great river to its source. Suddenly he stopped. Shucks, he wasn't Meriwether Lewis. He was William Clark! Clark had red hair. Big George said so.

Wes ran his fingers through his own dark red hair. Then he let out a whoop and raced home. William Clark wasn't the only redhead who would explore faraway places!

CHAPTER THREE

INDIANS AND GEOLOGY

The next morning when Wes arrived, Crookham joked, "You are an early bird! Don't tell me you're the fellow who gets the sun up!" Wes laughed and followed Big George to the table. "We covered a lot of territory yesterday," Crookham said, unrolling a map of Ohio. "But today we are going to stay right here at Jackson, in the extreme south-central part of Ohio. We're going to take a very small portion of this big country of ours and find what-all it contains."

Wes' eyes sparkled. "How do you do that?"

Big George led the way into the adjoining room which housed the museum collections. There were oak logs blazing in the fireplace to banish the last bit of morning chill. Lamps glowed in the shadowy corners. Wes looked around wide-eyed. From floor to ceiling, surrounding windows and the fireplace, the walls were lined with shelves. "Golly, you've got all sorts of things in here!" He moved to a table in the middle of the room. It was covered with stone and bone Indian artifacts. He pointed to one item but did not touch it until his teacher said he might examine it. "I know what this is! It's an arrowhead. Papa found several when he spaded the garden patch." He looked over the display of crude tools, a war club, moccasins, bowls, and woven mats. "You sure got a lot of stuff!"

Crookham snorted. "It's not *stuff*. It's all that is left to tell us of a once-powerful Indian tribe, the Eries. Every piece tells a story, if only you'll take the trouble to think about it."

Wes had seen the Indians who drifted into Jackson. They were ragged and dirty, and often so hungry his mother would not let them pass without giving them every scrap of bread in the house. Wes wrinkled his nose. "I don't like Indians."

Big George's chins quivered. "Never speak out of ignorance!" he roared. "How do you know you don't like Indians when you know practically nothing about them?" He puffed noisily as he moved toward a big chair by the fireplace. The legs creaked when he sat down, but didn't give way. Wes slipped onto a small stool. Crookham waggled a finger at his pupil. "Now you listen to me, young man! I'll hear no remarks about your not liking Indians. I guess no one ever told you they were once a fine people!"

"No, sir," Wes answered, obviously not believing the last statement.

"I'm not going to have a bright boy like you growing up like the others around here, turning dogs on the Indians and despising them! Theirs is a marvelous story, once you take the trouble to study it. Did you know the Indian tribes had their own languages, and arts and crafts, and myths? Did you know they are skilled in many things the white man is poorer for, for not knowing?"

"But they massacred people!" Wes protested. Every frontier child had been reared to fear Indians.

"They were savage, yes. They massacred a lot of people. But someday you will know why they did this, and not condemn them entirely. We took away their land, Wes. Hasn't anyone ever pointed that out to you? This was their homeland. They were here hundreds of years before the white man. But the settlers wanted their land and drove them away. We killed off the game they needed for food and clothing. They fought back the only way they knew, but we finally conquered them. They were a fierce, proud people, and we made beggars of them!"

Stunned by every word, Wes could hardly breathe.

His teacher went on to tell him about the Eries, who had once occupied the south shore of the lake, and how they were exterminated by the Iroquois. He described how the Miamis from Wisconsin, the Shawnees from the south, the Delawares from Pennsylvania, and even the Wyandots from southern Canada had gradually migrated across Ohio to escape the white man's usurpation of their hunting grounds. Since he was very dramatic in his narration, Big George soon had Wes in tears over the poor Indians.

"Oh, here now," he said, embarrassed, handing Wes his handkerchief. "I didn't mean to make you cry. I get so all-fired mad when folks sniff at my Indian relics and call them *stuff*. I know to some they're just old scraps of bone and leather, but to me they're very precious." With a sweep of his arm Crookham pointed to the table displaying his collection. "Someday these relics I have gathered will be priceless museum pieces, because I am one of the few men in Ohio who is taking the trouble to preserve remnants of the first peoples to live in this region. Before the weather turns too cold, I hope to take you digging in an Indian burial mound near here. I thought you might like to help me add to my collection."

"I would!" Wes vowed, wiping his nose and handing back the handkerchief. "If we find lots of arrowheads, could I keep some?" Suddenly he had a wonderful idea. "Mama collects spoons. My sister Mary collects ribbons. Could I start my own collection of arrowheads?"

Crookham knew that young boys liked to gather all kinds of odd articles. Relieved that Wes' tears had dried, he chuckled and said owlishly, "I warned your mother not to be surprised at what she finds in boxes under your bed.

"But wait a minute! Before you decide whether you want to collect Indian relics, come look at some other things." He grasped the sturdy arms of the chair and heaved himself to his feet. Then he waddled over to the wall shelves, Wes at his side.

"Can you tell me what this is?" he asked, pointing to a stuffed, mounted specimen.

"A squirrel!" Wes exclaimed. Then he identified a beaver, muskrat, fox, and wolf. "Wolves still run in packs on the north shore of Lake Erie," Wes learned from his teacher. He looked at the beady eyes and lip curled back over cruel fangs. "Wolves scare me!" he admitted. Although Crookham would have let him, Wes would not touch the grimacing head or claws of a bearskin. "I bet Lewis and Clark were plenty scared the first time a bear jumped out of the brush at them!" Now that he was this close to what had been a bear, he saw how really dangerous it was. "Are there any bears in Ohio?"

"Not any more. The settlers killed them off years ago. In fact, a bearskin is pretty nigh impossible to procure these days," Big George told him. "Now let's move along here and see how much more you can identify. What is this?" One after another, Wes named correctly a wild turkey's wing, a deerhide, crow's legs, a robin's nest, a beehive, a water snake's skin, and many others. He knew red-oak leaf from red maple, beech from elm and tulip poplar. Gently he lifted the stuffed body of a cardinal from the shelf and stroked it. "You should hear the cardinals scold when I hoe too near their nests," he told his teacher. "The wrens and chickadees will talk back to me, but the cardinals always fuss."

Crookham had dried and pressed many wild flowers. Wes knew these also: yellow and purple violets, blue aster, clematis, dandelion, butter-and-egg. The "darning needles" and butterflies looked so beautiful that he had a hard time keeping his hands at his sides. And the insects! What frontier boy familiar with a hoe didn't know most of these! "But I never thought of collecting bugs," he exclaimed. "I can find lots of them right in our yard."

Next, Big George moved to a large partitioned box. "You should know a little about the composition of the earth's surface in this area," he said, showing Wes samples of clay, gravel, limestone, sand, coal, iron ore, and unrefined salt. He had Wes feel them, smell them, even taste them. Then he explained that some two billion years ago the earth was born, a small, hot ball in the universe. For eons of time it was alternately scoured with winds, flooded with water, and torn with volcanoes, gigantic upheavals, and fracturing of its crust. Mountains were thrust up, only to be worn down. Seas poured over the land, and billions of tiny marine animals' bodies were deposited, layer upon layer, to form deep limestone deposits. Then came the age of the glaciers, advancing and receding on the face of North America.

This was Wes Powell's first introduction to geology, the science dealing with the origin, history, and structure of the earth. Crookham purposely made it a very simplified introduction, so that his young pupil could comprehend something of the vast, complex subject. But it must have struck a spark in Wes' mind, because he rushed outside and scratched a hole in the ground. "This isn't just dirt," he exclaimed gleefully, letting the particles sift through his fingers. "This is ge-o-lo-gy!" He was entranced with the word.

A moment later he was back at Crookham's side. "Tell me more about geology!" he begged. But his teacher reminded him, "We're just sampling today, remember? We'll come back to it later if you like. Right now I have to get off my feet. It must be about lunchtime. Suppose we have a bite to eat and then I'll read to you."

The "bite" proved to be cold sausage, corn bread, a bowl of cottage cheese, pickled crab apples, more boiled eggs, raisin cookies and cherry tarts. Wes put a wedge of sausage on a piece of corn bread and chewed happily. He still was so excited that his stomach knotted up at times, but his growing boy's hunger would not be ignored.

After eating, Big George put on small gold-rimmed spectacles and read from Edward Gibbon's *The Decline and Fall of the Roman Empire*. This was very rough going for a nine-year-old, but the teacher took his time, reading a short while and then discussing what he had read until Wes grasped the meaning. When he felt that Wes had sat still long enough, he moved over to the bookshelves. He pulled down books detailing world history from the time of the Phoenicians to the drafting of the United States Constitution; books on the literature of Greece, Rome, and England; books on the classical languages, on almost every science known to man. "We'll dip into most of these eventually," he promised.

The late-afternoon hours were unusually warm. Mr. Crookham began to yawn. He had expected Wes to fall asleep while he was reading, but the lad had remained alert. He knew Wes had been up at daylight to do his chores before coming to the library. "It must be that driving desire to learn that keeps him wide-awake." Finally Crookham couldn't keep his eyes open. "I think we've had a long enough session for today. I don't want to wear you out."

Wes was about to say, "Please, don't stop!" But then he saw Mr. Crookham yawn for about the hundredth time. "All right. Will you read some more tomorrow?"

Crookham shook his head, "No, we're not going to do the same thing tomorrow. Remember, I said we would dibble-dabble around at first. Well, tomorrow we're going to do something entirely different. We're going on a natural-history excursion!"

CHAPTER FOUR

GEOLOGISTS ARE LIKE
SQUIRRELS

When Wes announced importantly that his teacher was taking him on a natural-history excursion the next day, Martha
and Mary tittered. "Silly, all Big George means is that he's
taking you on a picnic."

"It is not!" Wes insisted. "It's something diffrunt."

"Can I go?" seven-year-old Bram begged, but his mother
reminded him that he could not miss school.

Wes was introduced to a neighbor of Mr. Crookham the following morning. "This is Dr. William Mather. He is a surveyor
and geologist. You seemed to take such an interest in my rock
collection that I thought it would be nice if Dr. Mather joined
us today. He knows a great deal about rocks and shells and
fossils."

Wes cricked his neck to look at the tall, spare man. "Can you
tell good stories like Big — Mr. Crookham?"

Both men laughed. Dr. Mather pursed his lips. "Well, I don't
know about that, young man, but I'll try — if you're a good
listener."

"Is Wes a good listener!" Crookham boomed jovially. "This
youngster will sit for hours without fidgeting as long as you're
telling him a story or reading to him." Then he pretended to

29

whisper behind his hand, "Have Dr. Mather tell you about climbing the mountains out West and surveying a tributary to the Colorado River. He'll make your hair stand on end."

Wes raked his fingers through his unruly hair. It stood on end anyway, no matter how he sopped it down. In running all the way from his home to Crookham's, his shirttail had pulled out; he was perspiring; his short pants were damp from splashing through the creek. But he noticed that Dr. Mather's boots were scuffed, his shaggy tweed trousers had burrs clinging to them, and his vest pockets sagged. He was smoking a small red clay pipe. Big George had one just like it in his collection of Indian relics! Wes was so awed that he didn't say a word while the three rode in Big George's special buggy far out into the country.

But Wes was disturbed about something too. He was squeezed in between the two men, with his legs wound around a large wicker hamper. Apparently they were going on a picnic after all! His secretly held disappointment made him look woeful.

Noticing this, Dr. Mather fished around in his pockets and pulled out a white rock. "Do you know what this is?" he asked.

Yesterday Wes would have answered, "Oh, just an ol' rock, I guess." But his teacher had had him examine a piece of limestone, similar to this one, so he could answer proudly. "That's limestone. Big — Mr. Crookham told me —— "

"Go on, call me Big George," his teacher interrupted good-naturedly.

"Big George told me limestone was formed millions of years ago when Ohio was covered by water and billions of tiny sea shells were deposited, then cemented together by tons of pressure." Wes took a big breath. He felt so smart!

Dr. Mather was satisfied with the simple explanation. "You'll see lots of limestone today."

Sometime later they arrived at Salt Creek Gorge, where the bank on one side gave easy access to the creek running along the bottom. As they wandered up the creek, between the rising walls of the gorge, Dr. Mather explained that this gorge, or ravine, had been cut by the erosive action of the creek water. Such a ravine, from ten to over a hundred feet deep in places, gave scientists and students a chance to observe what the ground looked like beneath the surface. "See, the sides of the gorge are limestone." He took a small hammer from one pocket and tapped on a small protruding chunk. In a few seconds Wes saw the remnants of a shell inbedded in the rock. "We'll find a number of these today. If we're lucky, maybe a mollusk or two, and a *trilobite*, a primitive sea animal that lived millions of years ago."

At first Wes couldn't find anything but "rock." But after he got used to the composition of limestone, he was able to find a shell or two. "This is like a treasure hunt!" he called out happily. His two teachers nodded. They were absorbed in looking for trilobites. Big George found one and was so jubilant he shook all over like a bowl of jelly.

Later Dr. Mather said, "Do you understand, Wes? What you are looking at is not just dirt or rock but layer upon layer of the earth's *history*."

Wes nodded. He remembered what he had been told about ancient seas, and glaciers changing the face of the globe many times millions of years earlier. "I know it isn't just dirt. It's geology!" Now he understood why Dr. Mather was called a geologist.

Suddenly Dr. Mather stopped sucking on his old pipe. "Wes, did it ever occur to you that squirrels and geologists have a lot in common?"

Wes didn't know whether the eminent scientist was serious or not. "You're funning me," he said, his gray eyes twinkling. "Is that a riddle?"

"I'm serious." He knelt down at Wes' side and pulled a hickory nut from his pocket. "If you were a squirrel, what would you do with this?"

Wes took the nut between his hands. Then he worried it with

his teeth, as a squirrel would. "I'd bite and bite until I broke through the shell and found what was inside."

"Exactly! Now tell me how a geologist is like a squirrel."

Wes thought and thought. He chewed his thumbnail. The geologist had told him how he could "read" the story of the formation of Salt Creek Gorge by tracing and identifying the sedimentary layers exposed by erosion. Wes had watched both men pick up gobs of dirt and, after tapping them, find a shell or mollusk inside.

Suddenly Wes had the answer to the riddle. He almost jumped for joy. "You mean, a geologist is kind of like a squirrel because he's always wanting to find what's under the shell, the earth's shell!" He fidgeted excitedly. "You mean, geology is like the nut inside the shell. It's the meat of the earth's story."

Dr. Mather hugged Wes. "You're a smart lad."

Then Big George carried the lesson a step further. "Did you ever know a squirrel to be satisfied with one nut?"

"Oh no, sir! Squirrels run all around, sometimes two or three miles from their nests, looking for acorns and other kinds of nuts." Wes paused, and the idea that Crookham had hinted at came to him. "You mean, geologists are like squirrels because they start hunting near home and then keep going farther and farther away to find what they're looking for."

Big George nodded.

"Is that why you went out West?" Wes asked the geologist.

That was one reason, Dr. Mather admitted. His actual work kept him in Ohio. He was hired by the state to track down deposits of salt, coal, iron, fine clay for pottery factories, marble quarries, and other ground resources that could be developed commercially. "But curiosity drove me West," he confessed. He traveled at his own expense to St. Louis and joined a party of trappers and prospectors so he could journey to the Rocky Mountains and see the deep gorge worn by many rivers. "Although I saw only the most accessible part, I had a glimpse of the mile-deep canyon of the Colorado River, where there is more geology exposed than any other place in the nation, I believe. Someday if you want to see the very oldest rocks, how this old earth looks deep down to the beginnings of its creation, visit the Grand Canyon of the Colorado.

"We geologists haven't begun to discover the whole story yet, because we haven't been able to explore all of the Colorado from its headwaters to the Gulf of California. That's because the Colorado is the wildest, toughest, most secret part of our country. I know," he mused wryly. "I tried to crack the shell of the Colorado and didn't even make a scratch. But someday someone will succeed, and then all the blank spaces in the maps and science books will be filled in."

"Golly, would I ever like to do that?" Wes breathed wonderingly. He took a deep breath and exhaled slowly. "But I guess you would have to know an awful lot about geology first, wouldn't you? So you would know what to hunt for, and what it was after you found it?"

Crookham took his hand. "Yes, and the best place to start learning is right here in Salt Creek Gorge. Shall we continue our geologizing?"

"Geologizing? Is that what we're doing?"

"Yes. Geologizing. We are making a geological investigation of Salt Creek Gorge."

The word burned in Wes' brain. He was geologizing. That was very important. Only smart people did that. He strutted along the creek bottom.

At midday Big George returned to the buggy and opened the hamper. The picnic had all the proportions of a banquet. Wes ate to the bursting point. The two men lay down in the shade and slept. Wes stretched out and started reviewing all he had learned that morning. A few moments later he was sound asleep.

During the afternoon the three moved on to an Indian burial mound. They spent hours digging carefully for relics, sifting every handful of dirt in the process. When they finally decided to return home, Wes' shirt pocket was filled with arrowheads and a piece of an old pipe. He had started his first collection!

Once home, Wes raced into the kitchen and emptied his pocket's contents onto the kitchen table. His mother was interested but added, "Darling, be sure and keep those out of reach of the babies. You can tell me more about them later. Right now it's milking time."

Mary, who was thirteen and liked to show off what a persnickety housekeeper she was learning to be, scolded, "Get those dirty things off the table, John Wesley Powell!"

Wes laughed. After tucking them in a safe place, he hurried about his chores.

Month after month of specialized teaching passed in the library-museum, followed by more field trips. The geologist told him many stories about the fabulous mountain country of the West. He also taught him the simplest rudiments of the professional methods of surveying and geological exploration. Big George continued to open the wonderful world of natural history, the world that had always existed at the doorstep, in the yard, in the garden, on the path to the barn. With each session at the library the circumference of Wes' knowledge pushed out into many new frontiers.

Crookham had guessed rightly about Wes' becoming a collector. He filled box after box of specimens and stored them under his bed. Although he could not neglect his chores, he learned to look for a different flower, beetle, feather, nest — anything and everything that could be picked up, examined, and brought home from trips to the barn, pasture, and woodlot. But there were limitations!

One day on his way home from Crookham's, while the weather was still warm, Wes found a small water snake and tucked it in his shirt pocket. At the supper table, Mrs. Powell and the children bowed their heads while grace was offered, it being Wes' turn. He leaned against the table, hands folded, eyes squeezed shut as he concentrated on his prayers. Meanwhile the snake popped its head above the pocket, wriggled hard, and fell onto the table. It slithered between the platter and sugar bowl. Mary should have had her eyes closed too, but she was peeking to see that no one grabbed her favorite piece of corn bread. She saw the snake, let out a screech, and jerked back so hard that the tablecloth went with her. The plate of corn bread crashed to the floor. Her brothers and sisters laughed; even the infant Nell banged noisily on her highchair tray.

"John Wes-ley Powell!" His mother eyed him severely. At the same time she bit her lip to keep from laughing.

Wes rescued the snake and put it outside.

"Mama, he's got to stop collecting!" Martha complained. "You should see what I have to haul out from under his bed every time I sweep."

Bram piped up, "He has a dead mouse up there now, and does it smell!" He rolled his eyes and pinched his nose.

After calmness had been restored, Mrs. Powell said, "John Wesley?"

"Yes, Mama."

"No more live things in the house."

"No, Mama."

"No more dead animals, birds, snakes, or rodents in the house."

"No, Mama."

"If you must collect things, put up a shelf or cages in the barn."

His mother wasn't going to make him stop collecting! Wes' cheeks glowed. But he said obediently, "Yes, Mama."

"Now repeat the grace properly. Then let us have our ham and beans before they get any colder."

Reverend Powell did not deal as lightly with Wes' collections. He made him throw out "every piece of that heathen trash!" He made him reread *The Lives of the Saints*. At first Wes was heartbroken, but in a short while his sunny nature asserted itself. "After all, it wasn't a very good collection," he told Bram. "It didn't tell a story. It didn't mean anything to anyone but me."

Suddenly he realized, "I can start all over again and do better!" He wished he didn't have to plow through *The Lives of the Saints*. He would much rather read the pamphlets Dr. Mather gave him on snakes or birds or the structure of plants and trees. But his father made him return them and read only religious material at home. "You're going to be a minister," his father informed him. "I'll not have you wasting your time with this scientific falderal."

Each succeeding year there were more farm chores for Wes, strenuous ones, and time-consuming work. Somehow he remained lighthearted and burning with curiosity — despite his father's ranting that science and collections were "sinful."

Had Reverend Powell realized that these months of studying with Crookham and Mather would wean his son away from the ministry, he might have kept Wes at home. Fortunately he was gone weeks at a time, rallying the settlers to salvation and the cause of emancipation of the Negro. Wes had his share of fistfights, defending his father's and his own feelings about slavery. Even jovial George Crookham was threatened to stop arguing for freedom of the Negro or suffer the consequences. Feeling became so bitter in Jackson that one day the Reverend, Crookham, and Mather were attacked by a mob in broad daylight. They were forced to take refuge in a nearby house, and when the rabble-rousers withdrew, they fled to their homes.

Late that evening the Powells heard someone shouting outside. They recognized Big George's voice and unlocked the door. He burst into the kitchen, crying, "The hoodlums have burned down my library and museum. All my books, my collections, my manuscripts are destroyed!" He collapsed into a chair and mopped his purple face. "I'll never live long enough to build it all up again."

The Powells were deeply shocked. Wes looked as if a horse whip had been lashed across his back. He stood by wordlessly, tears streaming down his face. Of the entire family, only Wes could really appreciate the great loss George Crookham had suffered.

When the big man had calmed somewhat, he brought Wes within the circle of his arm. "Wes, never let ignorant people stop you from what you know is right. Keep on plugging, forcing the truth on them. They'll hate you for it, but someday you will have your reward. If I've taught you only one thing, let it be this: "Go out in the world and discover as much truth as you can and then spread that truth as far as you can!"

Wes promised. He understood what his friend was asking of him: That someday he teach others as Crookham had taught him — opening people's eyes and minds to the wondrous discoveries as yet unrealized as the natural heritage of a sturdy, growing nation.

CHAPTER FIVE

ON HIS OWN

Wes had little time to grieve. In September, 1846, Reverend Powell moved his family to Walworth County in southernmost Wisconsin because he was pledged to minister to the outlands and Ohio was no longer a frontier. The new home was in a clearing surrounded by clumps of burr oak. As soon as the wagons stopped, Wes, twelve now, and Bram, ten, ran to the brook, scaring up quail and prairie chickens along its banks. "I'm glad we're going to live in the country," Wes told his brother. "Big George said I'd find lots of new birds and plants in Wisconsin." He rolled up his pants and waded in the water, Bram right beside him.

The boys' moment of freedom was soon over. Reverend Powell whistled them to start cutting firewood. Mrs. Powell and the girls inspected the rickety cottage built by the former owner, and decided it needed a thorough cleaning. Everyone pitched in, wielding mops, brooms, and hauling trash. Even four-year-old Walter did his share by tending baby Juliet. By nightfall the Powells were under their new roof.

The next day the Reverend rode to a nearby village to purchase two cows, some chickens, pigs, and sheep, and cuttings of grape, plum, and apple trees. Later he and the boys planted spring wheat, corn for the livestock, and hauled wagonloads of vegetables from the village market. Mrs. Powell set out her day lilies and other bulbs brought from Ohio. Wes and Bram made a holiday of scouring the woods for wild berries for preserves. Their father did not begin his ministerial work until his family was well provided against the coming winter.

One evening Reverend Powell announced that he must begin devoting all his time to spiritual matters. "I'm turning over the entire management of the farm to you, Wes," he said. Since his father's word was law, twelve-year-old Wes didn't argue. However, Mrs. Powell, who rarely questioned her husband's decisions, protested. "Joseph, you can't mean that! Wes is too young. He's not strong enough to do the heavy work."

After some discussion the Reverend agreed to hire a man when absolutely necessary, but insisted that Wes shoulder the over-all responsibility. Wes was given no say in the matter. He was expected to do as he was told.

In the following months Wes and Bram and the older girls felled trees, pulled stumps, broke prairie sod for crops, dug ditches, rooted out weeds, and in their spare time built a chicken roost, pig pens, and a threshing floor in the barn. Mrs. Powell and the younger children tended the large vegetable garden. It was back-breaking labor, perhaps too much, because Wes expended so much energy in farmwork that there was scant left over for growing. Somehow he found time to enlarge his small knowledge of nature by studying the new shrubs, trees, and weeds, calling to strange birds, and in wintertime hunting the snowy trails. There were no ravines nearby so he made no progress in geology. He found many things he could not identify, and with no adequate text to guide him, he hungered for knowledge.

The girls were airing quilts one sunny spring day when they spied a band of Indians setting up camp by a big spring not far from their home. They screamed and ran to the house. Mrs. Powell, alone as usual with her brood when an emergency arose, barred the doors and peeked nervously through the window. After her first fright wore off, she noticed the Indians didn't look very menacing. They were ragged, obviously weary, more like the stricken wanderers who begged bread at her Ohio door.

Suddenly there was a pounding on the kitchen door. The girls were terrified, but Mrs. Powell realized that it must be the boys, who had been working outdoors. She hurried to let them in.

After hearing about the Indians, Wes studied them from the window. "They're hungry. See, their cookfires are smoking. They'll be up here pretty soon to beg."

Mary burst into tears. "I don't want them near the house. They'll set fire to it and kill us!"

Wes snorted. "Scaredy-cat! Those Indians aren't going to hurt us. They aren't dangerous. They've got all the fight knocked out of them. Big George said so." He faced his mother. "I'm not afraid of them. If you don't want them coming to the house, let me take a sack of bread down to their camp."

Mrs. Powell peered out the window again. "Are you sure, son? If anything happened to you — "

Wes insisted. "Honest, I won't have any trouble."

By this time Mrs. Powell was convinced that the Indians weren't dangerous. She filled one sack with bread and another with vegetables. The family crowded around the window to watch slight, barefooted Wes make his way down the trail, the sacks bouncing on his shoulders. When he reached the camp, the squaws fought over the food like dogs over a bone until the chief quieted them. The whole tribe had learned an English jargon in their wandering, so Wes was able to converse a little with them.

The younger boys stood in the background, scowling until he marched up to them and said, "Anyone want to go fishing?"

Fishing meant food and fun, so the boys agreed. While they stripped willows for poles, Wes learned that they were Winnebagos, once a fierce tribe, now miserable beggars. The boys told him the village was on its way to Chicago to talk to the "annuity mans," the federal authorities who would pay them in

cheap calico, blankets, and other trifles for the valuable farm-
land they had surrendered to the government.

Fishing was good. When there was enough for every family,
Wes showed the boys a cache of green acorns and a wood-
chuck's hole. Remembering what Big George had said about
Indians being fine people if you knew them, he asked many
questions. The boys told him how their grandfathers' grandfathers had roamed the prairie that was now called Wisconsin,
had hunted and fished and staged rabbit drives. They told him
legends about the big spring nearby, the tall oaks, about the
spirits they worshiped. What Wes learned made him want to
be real friends. He accepted an invitation to eat with the boys.
Afterward the grownups sang and danced for their new friend,
but all too soon it was time for Wes to trudge homeward.

As he entered the kitchen, he found his mother knitting by
lamplight. Eyes shining with excitement, Wes told her about
the Winnebagos. At first Mrs. Powell listened attentively, but
suddenly she shrieked, "Lice! You're crawling with lice! Out to
the trough with you!"

Wes hadn't minded the lice, but he did mind having to jump
in the cold water fully dressed. His mother used strong homemade soap on his head until his scalp burned. Then Wes had to
scrub himself and wash his clothes. He shivered as he hung his
clothing to dry because the night air was cold. It was good to
return to the warm kitchen, slip into a clean nightshirt, and
have a bowl of corn bread and milk before going to bed.

The Winnebagos moved on at daylight, and Wes had to work
fast to catch up with his chores. About ten days later they returned, the women gaudy in their cheap cotton dresses, the
men shouldering sleazy blankets, the children kicking stones
with their new shoes. Now there were new tents set in a circle,
much singing and dancing, and plenty of coffee and beef. However, the next morning the campsite was deserted again. Wes
never saw these Winnebagos again, but he never forgot them.
From a few things they had given him, he started a new collec-

tion of artifacts. The boys had located an old burial ground for
him and here Wes found many more. These he labeled carefully, as Big George Crookham had taught him.

During the first year in Wisconsin there was not enough
wheat harvested to market. But the second and third year, with
many more acres producing and the threshing floor completed,
Mrs. Powell and her children readied three hundred bushels.
Their jubilation was short-lived. The Reverend was too busy
working away from home to haul the crop to market. Once
more his wife and children had to face an emergency on their
own. The nearest market was a four- to six-day journey over
terrible roads. Mrs. Powell couldn't take the entire family, and
it was unthinkable for unmarried girls to travel by themselves
or be left at home without an adult. Wes saw the problem and
volunteered to go.

Mrs. Powell's workworn hands caressed her son's bony shoulders. She sighed deeply. If only her husband weren't so occupied with other people's spiritual welfare! A thousand dreadful
fears crossed her mind. Wes could be cheated or robbed, even
killed!

Sensing her worry, Wes said, "Nothing's going to happen to
me. I'd like to go to market."

"We'll pray hard every minute for your safe return," Mary
exclaimed, as she nervously twisted the corner of her apron.

"I'll do your chores," Bram offered.

Mrs. Powell finally agreed. "All right, you may go."

She told Wes how to bargain a good price for the wheat,
which represented the family's entire cash income for the year.
He was warned about ruffians and bandits. He was told how to
buy yard goods, needles, spices, medicines, how to shop so that
he wouldn't be cheated. "If you see a book you've been wanting, and it doesn't cost too much, buy it," Mrs. Powell told him.
Wes grinned. No job was too tough if the reward was a book.
He wanted badly a book on animal and plant structure.

Wes discovered many wagons on the road to Southport, the

nearest market. Most of the drivers were hired men — rough, foul-tongued, roistering brawlers. Yet at night they invited him to camp near their fire ring, and saw to it that no one molested this slight, red-haired youth.

Although only fourteen, Wes bartered a good price for his wheat and shopped carefully for his family's needs. On this first and succeeding trips, he enjoyed the grain and livestock auctions, the gay market place, the band concerts, and the harvest festival. He met William Wheeler, a scholarly, devout young man of twenty-one who loaned him books to read on the long ride to and from town. The two became close friends. Wheeler was surprised that Wes preferred adult books and could discuss many subjects intelligently. He located a good botany text that Wes could afford to purchase. Again and again Wheeler urged Wes to go to college, no matter how much drudgery had to be endured to achieve this.

Wheeler became Wes' idol. When he said, "I think mineralogy and chemistry are the two great fields of development in the future," Wes positively glowed. Mineralogy? Wes knew minerals were more apt to be found in mountain country. Why, mineralogy was first cousin to geology! Mineralogy fairly shouted mountains to a lad who had not forgotten what Dr. Mather had told him about the far West. "If I go to college, I'll study mineralogy," Wes said stoutly.

Although he didn't tell his family of his decision, Wes did talk about William Wheeler. Reverend Powell, home for a brief period, wanted to meet his son's companion. Martha and Mary, intrigued by their brother's description of the handsome young man, had a hard time hiding their excitement. On the next trip home from market Wes was accompanied by his new friend.

Mrs. Powell liked William Wheeler because he was clean and had nice manners. The girls fairly swooned over his good looks. The Reverend cross-examined him on his religious beliefs and found nothing to criticize. After supper they all gathered around the piano to sing. Wes, always bright-eyed and observant, noticed that William couldn't take his eyes off Mary, and she fluttered her eyelashes whenever her father wasn't looking.

Everyone was relieved when the Reverend invited the young man to call at the house as often as he could.

During the winter there were fewer chores to drain Wes' energy, so he spent hours working on his collection, classifying and labeling hundreds of items gathered around home as well as on trips to market, outland prairie, and forest. Since he had no money for mounting materials, he whittled his own pins and boxes. Bram liked to help with the museum, which was patterned after George Crookham's, but he couldn't get enthusiastic over the difference between a May beetle or a tiger beetle, the way Wes did.

Whenever the Reverend was home, he criticized the time Wes spent on his collection, and demanded Wes turn from such heathen pursuits and prepare himself for the ministry. Father and son couldn't be together five minutes without arguing. Month in, month out, Wes withstood the criticism. It washed over him as water over a creek bed, because more deeply impressed in his mind were George Crookham's and William Wheeler's words of advice — study science, go to college.

Outwardly Wes remained a happy, loving youth, thanks to his affectionate relationship with his mother and brothers and sisters. Inwardly his mind seethed with unanswered questions. He was starved for more knowledge to stimulate and inspire him.

Absorbed as he was in his collections, Wes took scant notice of a new situation in the Powell household that winter. William Wheeler became an increasingly frequent visitor but spent more time in the parlor with Mary than talking to Wes. Another likable young man, Joe Davis from Decatur, Illinois, was courting Martha. Toward spring only Wes, now working fifteen hours a day at farm chores, was not swept into the excitement of the coming weddings. Martha and Joe Davis were married first, the neighbors coming from miles around for the garden ceremony and celebration. A few weeks later Mary and William Wheeler were married.

Although summer was a time of almost 'round-the-clock work for Wes, he thought constantly of going to college. At first it seemed impossible. He was needed at home. Then, when he saw Lida and Nell take on Martha's and Mary's chores, he wondered if perhaps Bram, now a sturdy fourteen, could assume responsibility of the farm, as Wes had done at that age.

"It's worth a try," Wes decided. Without revealing his hopes, he began coaching his younger brother on how to manage the farm. Bram took to responsibility like a strong horse to a plow. He wanted to pull the load because it made him feel like a man. That fall Bram was allowed to go to market with the crop. When he proved dependable, Wes felt that the time had come to speak out. On his father's return home, Wes announced he wanted to leave and enter a school where he could prepare himself for college.

Much to Wes' surprise, his father not only gave his consent; he even offered to give Wes some money toward his expenses.

"Really, Father?" Wes exclaimed happily. This was too good to be true!

"Yes," Reverend Powell assured his son, "providing you study for the ministry."

Wes' small hope died. "But you know I want to study science!" he protested.

"Drivel!" the Reverend exploded. "How can you have so little concern for the salvation of your soul?" He pounded on the table. "It's God's will that you study for the ministry!"

"It is not God's will!" Wes dared answer. "It's your will, your selfish, domineering will that won't tolerate any ideas but your own! . . . If I studied for the ministry to save my soul, I'd be a hypocrite. I'd hate myself!" Wes jumped to his feet, pleading for understanding. "A man has to be true to himself, father, or rot inside. You experienced a divine calling to preach. I haven't. I — I feel called to dedicate myself to science. Can't you see that a man doesn't have to be a minister to serve mankind? I want to serve my country. I want to help people. I promised Big George to bring the truth to them. But I have to do it my own way, through science."

Reverend Powell would not listen. "If you leave this house to study science, I'll not give you one penny's help. And may the Lord forgive you for deliberately choosing a heathen's career!" he thundered.

Wes looked down at his strong, work-gnarled hands. He was sixteen and had done a man's labor for years. He had had little help from this demanding, intolerant man. For four long years he had been denied any schooling. Now, far from being discouraged, Wes found a new confidence born within him. He felt absolutely no fear about facing the future on his own. Thus he was able to say determinedly, "I'll go it alone."

The next morning, warmed by his mother's and brothers' and sisters' loving farewell, John Wesley Powell walked out of the house, across the clearing, through the oaks, and on to the open road. His footsteps did not lag as he headed for Janesville, some twenty miles away. There was a school there, and through its doors Wes hoped to enter a new world of learning and adventure.

CHAPTER SIX

SCHOOLMASTER

The school at Janesville would have discouraged anyone but knowledge-hungry Wes Powell. It was a dingy, one-room shack, the teacher poorly trained. However, he was quick to point out the new student's deficiencies in grammar and mathematics. "You're a long way from being ready for college."

"How soon can I start?" Wes asked, refusing to be disheartened.

The teacher sighed. He had forty pupils, all younger than Wes. He wasn't too happy about setting up a course of study for one advanced pupil. "Come back in a day or so," he said indifferently. "I'll have to dig up some books and outline your lessons — if you're really interested," he said.

"I'm interested," Wes assured him, promising to return after finding a place where he could work for his room and board. The first farmer Wes approached hired him on the spot. He was to care for the cattle and sheep and do the maintenance jobs, but have the entire day free for school and studying. It meant long, hard hours, but Wes was used to this. During the winter nights he studied by firelight. When the farmer and his wife went calling, Wes rocked the cradle with his foot and did his geometry with a toddler asleep on his lap. He was reasonably content. At least he was making some progress, thanks to his own persistence and the lackadaisical assistance of the instructor.

At the end of the first semester Wes was dismayed to receive a letter from his father telling him to return home. Reverend Powell had sold the Wisconsin farm at a good profit, thanks to the improvements made by his hard-working wife and children. He had purchased three hundred and twenty undeveloped acres at Bonus Prairie, in Illinois, and wanted Wes to drop his studies and "put the new farm in order."

For a moment Wes ached to refuse. More than anything in the world, he wanted to keep on with his schooling. But when he thought of the back-breaking work facing his mother and younger sisters and brothers, he told himself, "They need me. I've got to return." He packed his books, but not without promising himself that he would keep on studying. He said good-by to the farmer who was sorry to lose him. "You're the hardest-working helper I've ever had," he complimented Wes.

Once more Wes took his place as manager of the family farm. If he resented the highhanded way in which his father profited from the family labors and did not hestitate to plunge them into further difficult toil, Wes kept this feeling to himself.

His mother saw to it that Wes' evenings were free for studying. Somehow, out of the deep core of strength, he found time to make word games lively at the supper table. He read to the family while the older girls did the dishes, Bram strained the night milking, and his mother "set down" the sponge for the next day's baking. For a brief respite, all joined in family singing. But long after the others were asleep, a small lamp glowed on Wes' makeshift desk, or a candle sputtered on the bedside shelf. "I'm so ignorant!" he often cried out in anguish. "There's so much I don't know!"

After the family was well settled in Illinois, the prairie broken and crops planted, Reverend Powell said, "Wes, you are a good son. I do appreciate all that you have done. As a reward, I'll pay your tuition at Oberlin, providing you study for the ministry."

Wes had long dreamed of attending Oberlin, the great liberal college in Ohio. He could have compromised. Common sense told him it was the only way he would be able to complete his studies and be awarded a degree. However, his love of science and his personal fortitude were so strong that he found courage to refuse. That precipitated further bitter arguments with his father on the subject of religion versus science.

Fortunately Reverend Powell soon departed on his outland ministry, and Wes could study in peace. Grammar, advanced mathematics, logic, philosophy, geography, and biology all drew his attention. Before long he realized that he knew more than the teacher at Janesville. One night he had an idea. It made him sit bolt upright. "I wonder if I could qualify for a teacher's certificate! Maybe I could earn some money teaching!" A hundred exciting possibilities crowded his mind. Gradually he sorted them out and made plans for the future. As usual, he said nothing to his family.

First he made sure that Bram could manage the new farm. After harvest time Wes walked thirty miles to present himself for examination by the district superintendent of schools. After the ordeal of written and oral tests were over, Wes could scarcely believe his good fortune. He was awarded his certificate and hired to teach in a one-room school at the whopping salary of fourteen dollars a month!

"With that much money," he rejoiced, "I can save a hundred dollars for college tuition in no time at all!"

The day before classes were to start, the eighteen-year-old teacher visited his classroom. It was a drab, dusty place with split logs for seats and desktops. Undismayed, Wes pitched in. He found a mop and broom, heated pump water over a fire, and scoured the place from rafter to door. Corners were brightened with fall foliage. Mottoes and maps were drawn with colored chalk to frame the peeling blackboard.

The next morning the smiling schoolteacher, standing tall in his threadbare suit and clean shirt, greeted his pupils and seated them at their grade levels. Devout John Wesley Powell started every schoolday with prayer. Late-comers found themselves locked out until the prayer was finished. Wes followed the prescribed outline of study, but several times weekly his classroom methods were those of George Crookham. History became a dramatic story acted inside or out of doors. Napoleon's defeat at Waterloo came alive as students lined up as opposing armies, the primary pupils recruited for flagbearers and trumpeters.

Farm children, who took insects and weeds for granted, were introduced to the vast fascinating world of natural science when their teacher, infecting them with his own enthusiasm, led them on periodic field trips. Scarcely a day passed without something new being added to the collections now lining the once-barren walls.

Soon the parents became interested. "Could you have at least one night class weekly devoted to lectures for adults?" they asked the young schoolmaster.

Wes swallowed hard. "Gosh, I don't think I know enough." He took a deep breath. "But I'd sure like to try!" Here was a challenge he wanted to meet. He began by discussing natural history and geography and reading from some new pamphlets on irrigation and land use. Before long, young people from neighboring villages came to hear "Professor" Powell. Actually the classes helped Wes because he benefited from adult-level discussions that made him think on a more mature level.

A year's teaching did a good deal more for him. He discovered that he liked people of all ages and interests. He burned with the desire to enrich their lives through the new knowledge he could bring them. He found it very easy to fulfill his promise to George Crookham. Having to plan studies for young and adult groups taught him to be orderly and logical. He learned to speak effectively, with poise far beyond his years. He was friendly, full of optimism and confidence, and completely self-reliant. Years of farmwork had made him sturdy and tireless.

Although the school year passed in a glorious frenzy, Wes never lost his secret yearning to go to college. He still took time to increase his knowledge of the required subjects. Very practically he looked upon these months of new experience as a great adventure, rather than as a delay in his long-sought hope.

Unfortunately his expenses were more than he figured, and summer found him with too few dollars saved. Returning home to help with the farm, Wes learned that his family was considering another move. Reverend Powell had helped establish a new college at nearby Wheaton, Illinois, a few miles west of Chicago. He wanted his family moved there so the children could have continuous schooling. When Wes realized that moving to Wheaton meant that he could go to college and also live at home, he pitched in wholeheartedly.

Eleven years had passed since five Powell children had enrolled in their first school at Jackson, Ohio. Now six Powells — Wes nineteen, Bram seventeen, Lida fifteen, Nell thirteen, Walter eleven, and nine-year-old Juliet — were on hand December 14, 1853, when Illinois Institute opened its doors to elementary, preparatory, and college students. All had been in a tizzy for weeks. Wes moved in a dreamy trance. He had waited and prayed and struggled for three years for this day to come. Illinois Institute might be a far cry from Oberlin, but it was a college.

When the registrar handed Wes the outline of study, he glanced impatiently over it. "Is this all?" he asked worriedly. "Aren't you offering courses in science or advanced mathematics or logic?"

"Not this first year," the man answered. "We are equipped only to give work toward teacher training and the ministry."

Wes let the outline dribble through his fingers. He stumbled out of the building. For hours he wandered about in the cold, overwhelmed with disappointment. Through his own efforts, he had already covered all the work the Institute offered. He didn't have enough money saved to enter another school. "But I'm not going back to farming! I'm not going to give up my dream of a college education!" he vowed grimly.

What could he do?

At nineteen, Wes swallowed his first bitter defeat. College was as far away as that day he had left the clearing in Wisconsin, determined to be on his own. "It's just going to take longer than I thought," he consoled himself. He would have to teach another year, scrimp and save, and maybe next fall the dream would come true.

Because of his fine record as a teacher, Wes had no difficulty getting an appointment to the Emerson School located on Long Creek about four miles east of Decatur, Illinois, and some sixty miles from his home at Wheaton. There were two bright spots in the picture: he would earn twenty-four dollars a month, and Bram would be with him to be tutored for college entrance.

The Emerson School soon buzzed with singing geography lessons and specimen-hunting field trips and a budding museum. A few weeks later adults were streaming to the schoolhouse after supper to hear the brilliant young schoolmaster lecture. In their free time Wes and Bram studied Latin and Greek, advanced mathematics, and science.

In the fall of 1855, when he was twenty-one, Wes finally had money enough to enroll in the science department of Illinois College at Jacksonville, in the west central part of the state.

"Oh, joy!" he greeted his new school. "I'm going to wallow in science!"

Although he had to work for his board and room, do his own laundry and mending, Wes still found time aside from his studies to join in student debates and the modest social activities. Others might kick up their heels square dancing, but not Methodist-raised Wes Powell. So he sat on the sidelines, his toes tapping in time with the fiddle, and chatted between dances with the gay couples. He liked ice-skating parties and taffy pulls. He was supremely happy, and busy.

Wes was not considered handsome. Because he was not too tall, he carried himself very straight and combed his thick auburn hair in a pompadour to give the appearance of added height. He was self-conscious about his rather prominent round nose that was always red from sunburn or frostbite, but friendly gray eyes, a mellow speaking voice and a warm outgoing personality added to his popularity.

Then in the spring a new resolve took hold of him, one that was to have a profound effect on his entire future.

CHAPTER SEVEN

ADVENTURE ON THE MISSISSIPPI

One afternoon in May Wes found his attention wandering during a lecture on plant-tissue cells.

"Collenchyma are the strengthening cells found in stems," the botany professor droned on, his pointer making small ticking noises as it touched a diagram drawn on the blackboard. "Please note the epidermal cells here, and —— "

Wes' seat was in the row next to the window, open now to admit the soft, fragrant air of a spring day. Birdsong smothered the pointer's ticks. On such a day as this long years ago he had gone to school out of doors with George Crookham and Dr. Mather. He remembered how he had sworn to be an explorer then, or at the very least to simulate a squirrel and venture far from home.

Wes squirmed on the hard chair. His big toes began to twitch. Soon his feet itched all over. He almost chuckled aloud, but stopped before he disgraced himself by laughing during a lecture on collenchyma cells. "I know what's wrong with me," he diagnosed this new feeling. "I'm coming down with 'Explorer Fever.'"

Instead of rushing to his room to work on a term paper that afternoon, Wes strolled to the edge of town. The full glory of spring thrust its color and music upon him. He lay down on the grass, hands under his head, and watched the clouds drift by.

It was so good to be lazy, to take time to dream!

What had happened to his child's notion of being an explorer, he asked himself. What had happened to his yen for collecting? His duties, both at home and school, had tied him down to the small world of daily living. He didn't have time for collections any more. Yet he realized that to be an effective scientist, he must travel, observe, and study areas beyond the small circumference of his present location.

For a moment he toyed with the idea of a walking tour out West, but quickly discarded the notion. "I'm not prepared well enough in geology to get much out of a trip to the Rocky Mountains. I'd better stick closer to home." Ideas drifted in and out of his mind. Suddenly he sat up and snapped his fingers. "Here I've got one of the greatest rivers in the world practically under my nose, and I haven't even seen it!"

His mind was made up. He would beg, borrow, or build a boat and row up the Mississippi to St. Paul. "I'll collect shells and mollusks, and study the flora and fauna along the bank. What a pipper of an adventure!" He was free to go now that the family lived in town and maintained only a large kitchen garden.

It took all the will power Wes could summon to finish out the term. He wrote home of his intentions and received an encouraging letter from his mother. Endearing messages were enclosed from his brothers and sisters. The Reverend maintained a disapproving silence.

The day that school closed, Wes stored his books and extra belongings and prepared his pack. In a canvas knapsack he put a change of clothing, sweater, rubber tarpaulin, towel, toothbrush, and bar of homemade soap. His "scientific tools" consisted of tweezers for handling small insects, a "geologist's" hammer, a dissecting knife, a magnifying glass, catching net, several textbooks, notepaper, and pencils. He added a small shovel and trowel, a long-handled skillet, a stew pan, his small-bore gun and ammunition. He walked the twenty-odd miles to the river and saw the broad, limpid stream from the Illinois side almost directly across to Hannibal, Missouri, on the west side.

After scouting around, he bought an old rowboat for very little money, recalked it, and fitted it up for his "expedition." He whittled sturdy oars and a watertight locker. He also made a plant press of several perforated thin boards held together with ropes, and a vasculum — a metal cylindrical container carried by means of a shoulder strap and used by naturalists to hold field specimens prior to examination or mounting. He spent a few more pennies for a sack of beans and another of corn meal, a little salt, and side pork. "I'll eat fish and quail and rabbit and berries," he promised himself. At last everything was in place. He stepped into his boat and was soon skimming along the comparatively quiet water of the shoreline.

Since Wes kept no diary, there is no written record of this journey. Only a few stories, passed on through the family, indicate what happened in the following weeks. That it was a dangerous journey apparently never bothered Wes. The east bank of the Mississippi was dotted with small settlements and outlying farms. But there were lonely miles where the river belonged solely to nature's children. Mile upon mile he ventured upriver, gleeful over his mounting collections.

Long before dawn each day he was on the water, observing birds, otter, muskrat, deer, cranes; netting butterflies and dragonflies; rocking the boat as he stretched to gather insects or leaves from overhanging boughs. Rain or shine, cold or heat, he worked, ate, and slept in the open, with the heavy, gurgling song of the river in his ears.

At that time the underbrush and caves on the banks were hide-outs for river pirates, the thieving, murdering scourges of barges, water-front towns, and pleasure steamers. One night Wes pulled his boat on a dry spit of land and made camp in the shelter of an overhanging bank. He was roasting rabbit meat on green willow spits, when two ruffians burst from the thicket and leveled their revolvers at him.

Wes froze but showed no fear. They were wild-looking creatures, filthy, bearded, roughly clad, as malevolent-looking as humans could be. If the intruders expected him to panic, they were disappointed. Wes knew they would probably rob him, though he possessed little of value. He could only hope they wouldn't kill him!

"Whatcha spyin' around here fur?" one asked belligerently.

"I'm not spying. I'm collecting shells and insects." He pointed to his day's harvest drying on the tarpaulin. "I collect butterflies too." An idea came to him. He grinned like a half-wit and said, "Have you seen a *papillo glaucus turnus* around here?"

"A what!" growled the other bandit.

Wes purposely looked hurt. "A pretty yellow butterfly with splotches of red and blue on its wings."

The ruffians eyed each other. They had seen at a glance that this was a poor outfit, with nothing much worth stealing. "He collects bugs!" one exclaimed.

His companion glanced at Wes, who did his best to appear addlepated. "He *is* bugs!" The robber made a circular motion with his index finger raised to his ear. "Let's get outa here."

"Maybe if I act like an idiot, they'll go away," Wes decided. His gun was out of reach, the knife small defense against two practiced killers. So he giggled crazily and said, "Don't you want to see the pretty bugs I caught today? I got some — " and he reeled off a dozen Latin names.

The bandits eyed him warily. It was bad luck to harm crazy people. Sometimes they could put a horrible curse on a man! "C'mon," one said to the other, and they disappeared into the brush with surprising little noise.

Wes' first impulse was to hurl everything into his boat and row away like mad. But he made himself stay by the fire, turning the meat and crooning an eerie song. It was a long time before his heart stopped pounding in his throat. As soon as it was completely dark, he moved on. After that he was careful to camp in open areas that afforded no hide-outs for pirates!

Wes also stayed away from towns. He had few coins left in his pocket, and he was interested more in natural history than in people. From the Illinois side he could see where the Des Moines River spilled into the Mississippi, and the white rapids across its mouth imperiled steamboat traffic. He passed above the area of low-lying alluvial mudflats into a portion where the banks rose in picturesque rocky bluffs, sometimes three hundred feet high. Still farther on, between Rock Island and Davenport, Iowa, there were additional cascades in the main channel, where the once-muddy river bed was now stratified limestone. Northward the Mississippi widened, flowing between the most beautiful valley farmlands Wes had ever seen.

At St. Paul, Minnesota, 1,150 miles above his starting point, Wes sold his boat and shipped home boxes of specimens. He walked briefly around the little town, then struck due east across the state of Wisconsin to Green Bay, following the shoreline of Lake Michigan south to Chicago, adding to his collections all the way. Nut-brown, thin, his clothing in rags, but as happy and free as a lark, Wes finally returned to Wheaton for a joyful reunion with his family. His mother and sisters clucked over him and stuffed him with rich food. Bram and Walter, now fourteen, tagged his every step. When Reverend Powell arrived for the usual brief visit, he showed small interest in Wes' adventures. Once more he tried to steer his oldest son toward the ministry.

"You might as well save your breath," Wes answered firmly but not impolitely. "I'm going to be a scientist."

"What kind of scientist?"

"I don't know yet," he admitted.

"You're twenty-two years old, and you still don't know what you're going to be?"

Wes turned away and left the room. He knew that other

young men his age were settling down and marrying, knowing and not fretting about the changeless routine that would be theirs for the future. But not John Wesley Powell. The vast, complex subject of natural history still pulled him in many directions. It might be years before he concentrated on one phase of scientific inquiry. Fortunately his boundless optimism soon washed out any feeling of guilt that his father's criticism had engendered. "I'm happy. I'm paying my own way. I'm learning every minute. That's enough for now," he decided.

During his second year at Illinois College, Wes worked at a dozen odd jobs to earn his room and board and spending money. He gobbled up the remaining courses offered in science. He mounted and catalogued his specimens and was proud to see them displayed in the college's small museum. The following spring of 1857 he faced a difficult decision. "If I get a farm job for summer, I might save enough to pay the fall tuition at Oberlin. But then I'd have to pass up an excursion down the Mississippi to New Orleans." He thought about and prayed on the decision for weeks. Finally he chose to spend the summer in solitary wandering into the Southland.

It was a choice he never regretted.

In another reconditioned rowboat he hugged the east shore and made good time, since he was rowing downstream. One bright June day he looked across to the mouth of the Missouri, where a raging, muddy red torrent poured across the clear Mississippi. Then two hundred miles further downstream he had to row frantically as he crossed the mouth of the mighty Ohio pouring its flood into the Mississippi. For the remaining 1,100 miles he followed the curves and loops, the narrow horse-shoe bends and meandering current of the lower river. Finally he half-rowed, half poled his boat past the salt marsh of the delta into the blue Gulf of Mexico.

The pattern of the previous summer was repeated. At New Orleans, Wes sold his boat and again shipped home boxes of specimens. Although the beautiful city intrigued him, he was more interested in the shells to be found on the shores of Lake Pontchartrain and the cypress swamps. He did not linger in the area, for New Orleans was just recovering from the horror of the great yellow-fever plague. Wes was no more confident than the townspeople that the scourge might not break out again.

By the time he returned to Wheaton, he was penniless. "But I've had a million-dollar excursion," he assured his family.

About this time Mrs. Powell had a great surprise. She received a letter from her brother, whom she had not seen nor heard from since leaving London twenty-six years before. Joseph Dean had migrated to the United States and was now living in Detroit, Michigan, with his wife and two children. He urged his sister to come for a visit. "Wes, will you go with me?" his mother asked. "I don't want to travel alone."

"I'd like to, if we can get back in time for me to apply for another teaching post," Wes agreed. Detroit would be new country. As long as he was without funds and did not have the money to enroll at Oberlin, he knew he must teach again. He had completed all the scientific courses Illinois offered and would not be returning there.

For some reason Wes assumed that his uncle's children were quite young. On arriving at Detroit, he was surprised and delighted to discover that one was an attractive girl only two years younger than he. Emma Dean became thoroughly entranced with Wes' stories of his adventures on the Mississippi. Wes liked her more and more when he realized how intelligent she was, and how free from the vapid silliness of most girls he had met. Besides, she thought science was "s-i-m-p-l-y wonderful!" Wes hated to leave Detroit. When he did, he and Emma promised to write often so that Wes could guide Emma in further studies of her new-found interest in natural history.

Without realizing it, Wes had slipped into a loose routine of study, teaching, and collecting trips. Secretly he hoped Emma wouldn't mind a long engagement.

In 1858 Wes finally reached his goal. He had money enough

to enter Oberlin. "I am studying Greek and Latin, and every course offered in natural history," he wrote home. He still found time to take part in impassioned debates on the issue of slavery versus emancipation. It bothered him when men said ominously that only a war could settle the mushrooming conflict.

However much Wes enjoyed Oberlin, apparently he was too restless to stay when spring drew him outdoors. Classrooms were too confining for a young man whose itch to travel now drove him eastward to seek out the sources of the Ohio. After that he floated down the river, having great fun collecting and imagining he was a latter-day Lewis and Clark.

In the fall he visited Emma and regaled her with tales of his travels. The two soon reached a secret understanding. "I don't mind waiting for you to find a job that will make you happy. But you must promise that, after we are married, you will take more field trips and take me with you," Emma said.

"I promise," Wes vowed.

Alas, Emma didn't realize what a restless man her fiancé really was! Three years passed, with Wes bounding from classroom to lecture platform, on to collecting trips and frequent geology field excursions. He toured Tennessee, Kentucky and Mississippi. He prepared an exhibit of 6,000 plants, another on shells. These were far more ambitious and better classified than George Crookham's and won various prizes.

Conchology, the study of shells, was all the rage among young ladies. Wes scoffed at those who made a dilatory hobby of collecting pretty things. His collections were arranged so that they made up representations of the shells to be found in the principal central United States' river-drainage systems. The same was true of his plant collections. Here again Wes was copying George Crookham. By means of these exhibits he brought hitherto-unrealized knowledge to others about their own towns and counties. He was widening their horizons, just as Crookham had brought fascinating new worlds within his comprehension.

Since he had taken courses in geology by this time, Wes felt prepared enough to lecture on the subject. Farmers, housewives, teachers, and young adults sat open-mouthed as he told them about the great depths beneath the earth's surface — how they were formed and what they contained. He led them to nearby ravines and creek banks and showed them, as Crookham and Dr. Mather had showed him, sedimentary deposits and evidence of the erosive work of wind and water. He made them see, as he had learned to see, that the earth's surface was not just soil or rock. It was a fabulous story of earth-forming stress and change going back billions of years. "This isn't just dirt," he told them, laughing as he scooped a handful and let it spill through his fingers, "this is geology!"

His listeners always chuckled when he said that. Geology! By cracky, there was real life in that word! Hearing it made a man want to stretch his legs outdoors and find out what had been going on these last hundred millions of years or so!

When Emma began to hope that perhaps her young man was finally ready to settle down to a steady teaching job so that he could support a wife, it was April, 1861. The entire nation was stunned by the news that the American flag at Fort Sumter had been fired upon by other Americans! The long-smoldering bitterness over slavery finally boiled over. America was faced with civil war.

When President Abraham Lincoln issued his first call for troops to defend the union, one of the first to volunteer at Hennepin, Illinois, was John Wesley Powell.

CHAPTER EIGHT

MAIMED!

On May 8, 1861, John Wesley Powell was sworn in as a private in Company H, 20th Illinois Volunteer Infantry. Enlistment was a speedy affair. The orderly jotted his name in the *Company Descriptive Book,* his age: "Twenty-seven, sir," and height: "Five feet, six and one-half inches." Wes would like to have stretched that figure a bit, but was truthful. In his platform appearances he had developed such a straight way of carrying himself that he gave the appearance of being taller. The orderly then added the information: eyes — gray; hair — auburn; occupation — teacher. Actually by this time Wes had advanced to being superintendent of schools at Decatur, Illinois, and was earning one hundred dollars a month. There was no column in the record book to write that he had a stylish beard covering most of his face and was well groomed, save for overloading his pockets with notepaper, stub pencils, and stray specimens. No note was made of his distinctive roundish nose, sunburned from a recent field trip. A doctor gave Wes a cursory examination and found him sturdy, though slight; he had no physical defects and weighed one hundred and twenty pounds.

Since his education was superior to that of most volunteers, Private Powell soon was elevated to a sergeant's rank, and a month later to second lieutenanet. His company was mustered into the United States service and moved to Alton, Illinois, for training. With his usual zest for learning, Wes got hold of some books on military science and engineering and crammed this new knowledge into his head. On his first furlough he went to Chicago to be fitted for a uniform. It consisted of an almost knee-length dark blue single-breasted dress frock coat sporting nine large eagle brass buttons, a stand-up collar, and cuffs edged with light blue welting. The regulation "trowsers" were baggy, unpressed, and spread well over his shoetops. Wes was proud as a peacock the day he slipped into new cotton underdrawers, pulled the gingham shirt over his head, secured the trousers with galluses, and then buttoned himself into the resplendent frock coat. He perched the soft blue forage hat atop his burnished hair and hurried off to Detroit so that Emma could see him in all this glory.

Emma had always scorned girls who had the "vapors" at times of emotional strain, but this time she melted into Wes' arms. It was all so thrilling, so romantic, that she couldn't help weeping. Although they spent as much time together as possible, reading poetry to one another or promenading Detroit's boulevards, their reunion was all too brief. Once more Emma gave in to tears as Wes boarded the train for camp. The two were deeply in love, and she would have to stretch her patience now that war was at hand.

On July 10 Wes' company went into camp at Cape Girardeau, a small settlement on the Mississippi bluffs not far below St. Louis. At first the days were crammed with drilling, handling of arms, and establishing a real military base. But as time passed and the soldiers found no Confederate troops threatening, their first excitement waned. They fretted through weeks of inactivity. Wes couldn't tolerate such idleness. As soon as his brief daily duties were done, he hiked off to the river front to collect shells, or scoured the woods for new insects and plants. He had no time for camp rowdiness. Specimen-collecting in a new area was more absorbing.

Noting his voluntary study of defensive tactics, Wes' superior officers instructed him to design and begin construction on works to fortify Cape Girardeau against enemy attack. In August, General John C. Frémont inspected the camp and personally approved Wes' plans, which called for four triangular forts connected by earthworks surrounding the entire town. The project kept Wes occupied for many months until General Ulysses S. Grant took command of the troops in southeastern Missouri. Since Grant wanted action, Wes soon found himself instructing men in artillery practice. On October 8, 1861, he was made a captain of artillery.

When General Grant revisited the camp in November, Wes spent three hours riding with him around the fortifications. Grant was so impressed that he invited Wes to have supper with him. Afterward Wes ventured to say, "General, may I ask a favor?"

General Grant, being in an expansive mood, answered, "No harm in asking. I can always refuse."

Wes didn't hesitate, though his cheeks flushed as he said, "Well, sir, I've kept a certain young lady in Detroit waiting five years. Emma is not exactly impatient, you understand, but I don't want to lose her for lack of taking action."

"You'll be seeing plenty of action very soon," the general interrupted.

"Yes, sir," Wes was quick to agree. A sudden shyness, quite contrary to his usual assurance, made him blurt, "Could I please have a week's leave of absence to get married, sir?"

Grant was secretly amused at the way this fine junior officer was suddenly all blushes. He puffed on his cigar for some time, while Wes almost suffocated from suspense. Suddenly the general smiled, extended his hand, and said, "I guess the war can wait a week, if your Emma has waited five years. Convey my personal best wishes to the young lady, Captain, and God bless you both!"

Wes jumped to his feet. "Thank you, General. May I be excused now, sir? I mean, if you've nothing more —— "

Grant's laugh boomed out. "Go on, go on. Write her the good news — but don't forget to report back here one week from today."

On the evening of November 28, in the presence of Emma's family and a few friends, the pastor of the First Baptist Church in Detroit performed the marriage ceremony. Immediately afterward Captain and Mrs. John Wesley Powell took the train for Chicago. There was a brief visit with Wes' family, and then the bride and groom traveled to Missouri, Wes to his army post and Emma to a room in Cape Girardeau.

Emma was divinely happy: married at last, and already traveling to new places with her handsome husband. But Wes had little free time to spend with her, although there were a few excursions into the country. General Grant's promise that there would soon be action was not an idle one. With a big offensive in the making, Wes spent long hours drilling and disciplining his men. He handled them well and received full cooperation because they soon realized that he had their welfare uppermost in mind. In March the troops moved to Pittsburg Landing on the west bank of the Tennessee River. Captain Powell, with his brother Walter serving as a second lieutenant under him, personally selected the campsite on the rolling tableland broken up with open fields, red-oak forests, and dense underbrush. The general's headquarters were at Savannah, a small town nearby. Emma moved there to be near her Wes, and once the camp was established, he had time for visiting. In spite of a deadly conflict brewing around them, the two spent idyllic afternoons hunting shells along the river.

What Grant and others did not know was that the battle shaping up was to be a bloody rout for the Union troops. Due to faulty preparations and ineffective reconnaissance, some 40,000 Confederate soldiers were able to approach dangerously close to the Union camp.

When the battle began, Wes handled his battery capably. After hours under blistering cannonading, just as he raised his right arm to signal, a Minié ball struck his wrist and plowed deep into his arm, almost to the elbow. Hurrying to his brother's aid, Walter saw that he was seriously injured. Walter applied a tourniquet and helped Wes to the shelter of a tree. Wes, meanwhile, was far more concerned about the battle and kept shouting, "Man the guns!"

Not long after, General Wallace rode by and, seeing the captain's shattered arm, advised, "We're almost surrounded. Take my horse and ride to the hospital boat at the Landing." He realized, as did Walter, that without quick attention Wes would bleed to death.

At first Wes refused to leave his men, but when Walter promised to stand by and the general virtually commanded him to ride, he left. Although almost blinded by pain and weak from loss of blood, he clung doggedly to the saddle. At the Landing he scarcely remembered being helped onto the boat. Through the entire distance he had ridden past the dead and injured, dying animals, hapless victims of a dreadful carnage.

The boat moved downstream to Savannah, where the litter cases were being transferred to a hospital, and here Emma was waiting. She nursed him and others through anxious hours. Wes' condition worsened, and the surgeon amputated the arm above the elbow.

Post-operative shock, fever, delirium — Wes' life was despaired of, but finally the crisis passed. Thanks to Emma's faithful nursing and his almost indestructible reserve of strength, he began to recover. But hard on the heels of this good news came his realization of the amputation. What a tragic blow to this man who had always dreamed of being an explorer!

Wes bore the maiming manfully — too much so, with too little outward rebellion. Emma knew that he was heartbroken. Slowly, with delicate understanding, she sought to help her husband to not only accept the loss of his right arm but resolve to surmount the handicap.

"If you'll just give yourself time to adjust," she begged, knowing full well that patience was one of his strong characteristics, "you can go on with your plans for the future. Maybe it will take you a little time to learn to do things, like dressing yourself or writing or mounting specimens, but I'll always be at your side."

At first Wes withdrew into himself. He, Wes Powell, one of the most independent men on earth, would have to be waited on hand and foot like a child! The thought was galling. "I won't accept help!" he vowed grimly to himself. During his convalescence he practiced, practiced, practiced — dressing, tying shoelaces, eating, writing. At times he struggled so hard that his face dripped with perspiration. "Did you ever try to comb your hair with your left hand? Or tie a shoelace one-handed?" he cried out, exasperation rawhiding him.

"You're doing better every day," Emma encouraged.

He spent hours learning to write with his left hand. One day he threw down the pencil and exclaimed disgustedly, "Look at that impossible scribble!"

Emma bent over the tablet, then kissed his cheek. "Oh, it isn't so bad, compared to your former handwriting. It used to take me hours to decipher your love letters!"

Wes blushed. "That was different. If I wrote badly then, it was because my emotions were involved."

Emma laughed. "The world is full of scribblers and scrawlers. Don't be such a perfectionist!"

One thing defeated him and he finally asked for help. "Emma, you'll just have to knot my tie."

His wife reminded him, "Don't I always fix your tie every day that we're together?"

This simple, devoted gesture did much to melt away the bitter wall of resentment and resistance that was building in a man normally happy and on good terms with the world. By degrees Wes accepted the fact that he would have to have help with some things for the rest of his life, that the assistance would be given lovingly by his wife, considerately by his friends, loyally by his associates in science. He must learn neither to begrudge it nor to think less of himself for having to accept it.

Another thing did much to straighten out Wes' attitude. A number of fellow officers and men who had served under him came to visit. After expressing sympathy over what had happened, they added, "We're looking forward to having you back with us, sir. We hope you're not considering taking disability retirement."

Wes sat up straighter.

The men went on to say that the Union had suffered heavy casualties and that the outlook for ultimate victory wasn't too bright. "Every able-bodied man must keep on fighting!" a young sergeant blurted out.

Able-bodied! They considered him able-bodied!

Wes looked himself over. Of course he was able-bodied. He had lost part of an arm, but the rest of him was fine! "Well, a little skinny, and weak in the knees right now," he admitted privately, "but I'll soon be as tough as a hickory nut." He had his legs and his sight; his thinking was unimpaired. Thousands were worse off than he. He realized that for the disabled, life would go on. Only the weak, the sour in spirit, would allow their afflictions to rob them of a full life.

"I'll be back in the traces in a week or so," he decided out loud, sounding very much like the old, vigorous Wes. Emma was so thrilled that she had to leave the room, lest he see her weep for joy.

His superior officer was glad to have him report back for duty. "We need you!"

Wes contacted General Grant by letter asking for a pass that would permit Emma to accompany him wherever he was stationed while serving the Army. Once more the general granted a favor.

From June 30, 1862, on, Wes served as recruiting, training, and supply officer in many areas, including forty days of extreme hardship fighting during the siege of Vicksburg.

Yet in the quiet periods the Powells found escape from the constant pressure of danger by hunting for shells. They gathered specimens at Memphis, Lake Providence, Richmond, Natchez, and New Orleans. Much of Wes' work was supervising the building of roads, bridges, and trenches. Incredibly, he could keep his senses alert simultaneously to two sciences: military engineering and natural history. He studied the rocks and fossil seashells uncovered in the construction. Box after box was mailed to his parents' home at Wheaton, Illinois.

All this was accomplished while Wes suffered constant and often excruciating pain in his wounded arm. In July, 1864, emaciated from lack of sleep, he was forced to undergo a second operation on the stump to gain some relief; it was fairly successful. While in the hospital he received a letter from army headquarters. After reading it he waved it at Emma. "Hooray, I've been promoted to chief of artillery with the rank of major in the Seventeenth Army Corps."

Emma almost swooned with pride. She hastened to write her family and friends that her husband was now Major John Wesley Powell. Hereafter Wes was known and addressed as "the Major." In their private moments Emma called him Wes, but otherwise, even to family and associates, she spoke of him as "the Major."

By January, 1865, with the progressive collapse of Confederate resistance, victory for the Union forces was so obvious that the Major finally gave in to his wife's pleas and requested a discharge from the army. Once this was accomplished the two left for Wheaton, for a family reunion "and a long, long rest for you," Emma mentioned hopefully to her thin, nervous husband.

The peace and quiet of the little town were soothing. Mother

Powell's cooking restored Wes' appetite, and he soon gained
weight. But two things goaded him. One, his youngest brother,
Walter, had been missing in action for many months. After a
lengthy correspondence, which was difficult for Wes, he located
his brother in one of the worst of the Confederate prisons,
where he was reported on the verge of madness from the dreadful conditions of his imprisonment. The news distressed the
family but Wes said, "I'm positive he'll improve as soon as we
get him home."

It took many more letters and months to negotiate Walter's
release. When he arrived, he was a rack of bones, moody and
disagreeable, yet pathetically glad to be reunited with his family. Once the nightmare of the prison camp was behind him, he
began to improve. Knowing that nature was one of the great
healers, Wes took Walter on leisurely walks out in the country.
They observed birds together, hunted for shells and insects,
observed the geological formation of the region. After such days
Walter was relaxed and tractable, but a few days' confinement
at home made him irritable.

"We're going to have to find some active, outdoor life for
Walter," Wes realized in time.

"You can do more with him than any of us," Mrs. Powell told
her oldest son. "He's happiest when he is with you. I don't know
what your plans are for the future, but try to help him, won't
you?"

"Of course," Wes promised, assuming this additional responsibility at a time when he was neither financially nor career-
wise able to support a wife and himself.

The second thorn in Wes' side was his own indecision. What
did he want to do? Should he try to specialize? What career
should be follow? He still didn't know!

His father reminded him, "Wes, you're thirty-one years old, a
maimed man with a wife to support. Get this nonsense about
science out of your head and settle down to teaching."

"Settle down!" Wes wanted to cry out, but he knew it was useless to argue. His father might as well have told him to stop breathing.

Inwardly he clung desperately to his big goal: Serve science. But he was too old to return to college, too exhausted by war and illness to be able to travel just yet.

In the following weeks Wes did a lot of thinking. It wasn't just "daydreaming," as his father insisted. Wes thought back over what George Crookham had taught him. He recalled Dr. Mather's talks about geologizing in the mountains and canyons of the far West.

Somehow, some way, Wes knew he had to go out there.

CHAPTER NINE

CLIMBING PIKE'S PEAK

Weeks later the Major was offered a professorship in geology at Illinois Wesleyan University, at an annual salary of 1,000 dollars. "I'm going to accept, not to quiet father's criticism, but because it offers me a chance to teach geology," he told his much-relieved wife, who was tired of living with her in-laws. Like any young housewife, she wanted a place of her own.

"The more I know about geology, the better prepared I'll be to profit from a trip out West," Wes figured to himself. His goal hadn't quite taken shape yet, but he sensed that this was a move in the right direction.

His geology classes were composed of seniors, alert, intelligent, full of enthusiasm, a stimulating challenge to their professor. Before long he and his students, and occasionally Walter, were scrambling over the countryside on field trips.

As if this were not activity enough, the Major and his faithful wife finished cataloguing the collections gathered during the war. They enjoyed working together, Emma tactfully refraining from being over-helpful. Weeks later they presented a truly magnificent collection of shells to the museum of the Illinois State Natural History Society which coordinated its program with Illinois Wesleyan.

At this time colleges throughout the country vied with one another in acquiring collections. It was their means of attracting

publicity and acclaim. Small wonder that the directors of the
Society became interested in a certain geology professor, particularly after laudatory articles on the shell collection appeared
in many Midwestern newspapers. But the Major was far from
satisfied. Although considered brilliant, even a genius, he well
knew his deficiencies. "I know a little about a lot," he confided
in his wife, "but I'm not a real scientist yet. I'm still dibble-
dabbling around. I'm an authority on nothing. I've got to study,
study, study!"

"If you need to study, do it. I'll study along with you." In
their cramped housekeeping rooms, Emma had arranged a study
area consisting of desk, bookshelves and work table. Her rocker
was as close to her husband's chair, without being in his way.
"Then when you make your trip West — " she continued.

Wes' eyebrows arched. "How do you know that I plan to go
West?"

Emma laughed. "Those itchy feet of yours won't be comfortable long in a professor's shoes. Besides, you promised to take
me to the mountains. Remember?"

Wes ran his fingers through his hair. "We don't have the
money."

"Money!" she chided him. "Use ingenuity instead."

After some thinking he said hopefully, "It means having to
scrimp."

"I'm willing."

"It means having to teach another year —— "

"And studying every free moment —— "

" — and drafting a thousand plans."

"We'll do it!" the two exclaimed simultaneously.

The Major bored into his heavy schedule the following year
with the intensity of a buzz saw. He taught courses in botany,
cellular histology, comparative anatomy, systematic zoology,
geology, mineralogy, and a night class for farmers on "Insects
Injurious to Vegetation."

Because of his outstanding work as a collector, the Major was named secretary of the Illinois Natural History Society. The directors would have been amazed had they known that they were falling in line with Professor Powell's long-range calculations. Wes, and the directors, knew that the Society could not gain prestige without evidence of some outstanding scientific work by one or more of its members. That meant collections. Collections meant travel. But travel cost money.

Once named secretary, Wes decided on an audacious plan. He marched to the State Legislature and held that body spellbound as he described the Society's need for money "for original research, for maintaining a museum whose collections could be loaned to other schools, for sponsoring a full-time curator to superintend the research and collections and correspond with noted scientists throughout the country."

The legislators granted an unprecedented 2,500 dollars, of which 1,500 dollars was for the curator's salary, the remainder for research, books, and "apparatus."

The Society showed its appreciation of this astonishing windfall by naming John Wesley Powell curator.

Curator!

Emma preened. Even Reverend Powell was impressed. The Major didn't care two hoots about the title — but was avid for the work connected with it.

"Now for the next step," he planned. "I must convince the Society to spend five hundred dollars for an explorative excursion to the mountain-park country of Colorado."

The board sat enthralled as the Major showed how he could make the Society's mediocre museum into the biggest and best in the Midwest.

He got the five-hundred-dollar appropriation.

"I'm still a long way from Colorado," he cautioned Emma.

"But look at the obstacles you've hurdled already!"

Wes took a deep breath. "We have a millon details to take care of before we're ready to leave." Unconsciously he spoke in terms of "we," much to his wife's delight.

The organization work towered like a mountain, but an eager Professor Powell was willing to toughen his legs surmounting it! Wes had learned many things in the army: how to handle men; how to circumvent, organize, substitute, and accomplish the impossible. Now all this valuable experience was grist to the mill of his ambition. He hied himself off to Washington, D.C., and succeeded in getting orders for rations for a party of twelve "to explore Indian Territory." An old friend who was now the Secretary of War, General Grant, signed the order. Next, Wes contacted various railroads and wangled free transportation for his men, then free shipping of equipment and specimens from the American Express Company and the Wells, Fargo Company.

"Isn't that enough?" Emma asked after he returned.

"No! I must have scientific instruments and more money." He asked several institutions to contribute one or the other, or both, promising in return to furnish them with a duplicate series of all but the rarest specimens gathered. He was not refused. The Illinois Industrial University (later the University of Illinois), the Chicago Academy of Sciences, and the august Smithsonian Institution chipped in.

Ingenuity was paying off handsomely.

Among his friends Wes found some willing to pay their expenses for the opportunity of exploring mountainous Colorado. Soon the Major had gathered a congenial, largely amateur, group of botanists, ornithologists, herpetologist, geologist, zoologist, and an artist. Unfortunately, Walter was still not strong enough for such an undertaking. Almon Harry Thompson, a young teacher who had married Nell Powell, would accompany them. Emma by now was an expert on alpine flowers.

By June, 1867, the preparations were completed. The Major saw the last piece of baggage tossed onto the train, then jumped aboard the coach that would take his shirttail expedition to Council Bluffs, Iowa.

There, on a high trestle bridge, the train crossed the Missouri

River. The Major pressed his nose hard against the window to see the yellow mudflats, the muddy river, and, on its west bank, the mushrooming town of Omaha. He could hardly wait to set foot on the ground. "It's been twenty-four years since I first determined to cross the Missouri." He was shaking a little. It was hard to believe that something he had dreamed of when he was nine years old had finally come to pass.

The expedition waited at the station briefly while the equipment and supplies were transferred to the wagons Wes Powell had arranged for weeks earlier. He assigned some of the group to handle the wagons, while the rest rode horseback. With Harry Thompson at his side, the Major led his little caravan due west toward the Platte River. Emma thought her husband looked so handsome astride his horse. He was lean-flanked, straight-backed, dignity personified in his second-best suit, light blue shirt, and string tie, his auburn beard glistening in the hot sunlight. Beyond the outskirts of town, dignity gave way to comfort. The Major shed his coat, then his tie, opened the shirt at the neck and tipped his hat back so he could feel the sun on his forehead. The others followed suit. Emma, perspiring under her linen dustcoat, resolutely clung to her broad-brimmed hat, veil, and gloves.

The Major chose the night campsite beside the Platte and supervised setting up the kitchen. He cleared ground space for his and Emma's bedrolls, then accepted help in raising his tent and securing the stakes and ropes. To celebrate the occasion, he decided to do what he had done the first evening of his two Mississippi River excursions: "I'm going to make biscuits."

He filled a large bowl with flour, sprinkled in a pinch of salt and soda, worked in the lard and water. On the tailgate of the cookwagon, he floured the breadboard, emptied the gray, lumpy dough onto it, and kneaded it, one-handed, with great gusto. There was just enough of a breeze so that the dough picked up a "flavor" of grit. Emma watched all this with sinking heart. When Harry Thompson laid too big a fire, she put the portable oven on the grate. Grinning widely, Wes slipped the pan of biscuits in to bake. They roasted, rather than baked, hard on the outside, gluey on the inside.

Not long after, he called out, "Come and get it! Our first supper on the road!" There was frizzled ham: "Fires burn so much better out here." And boiled potatoes, with hard centers: "Things take longer to cook out here." The coffee was lye-strong and full of grounds. The Major personally served the biscuits.

Harry Thompson tried to bite his, but thought better of his front teeth. After surveying his leaden, unappetizing portion he asked aloud, "Major, here is an interesting specimen. Cenozoic rock, d'you think? Clay or limestone?" He broke open the biscuit. "Still molten inside!"

Wes chuckled more like a young boy than the leader of a scientific expedition. "I'd say metamorphic rock, Harry. A very rare item, called *goodfordunkum*." He dunked his in the coffee and chewed reflectively. "Definitely sandy texture." The laughs were hearty. The biscuits were not wasted. Everyone enjoyed *goodfordunkum*, and the rest of the poorly cooked meal. "We'll improve," Wes prophesied. "A week from now we'll be as good as mountain men and forget that we were ever green dudes."

That evening just before sunset the Major and Emma strolled along the banks of the shallow, almost mile-wide Platte, the water molten gold reflecting the almost horizontal shafts of late sunlight. Although both were prepared for far-distant vistas, Wes remarked, "There's such a difference in reading about a place and actually seeing it. There's so much sky out here! Even the air has a drier, spicy smell that defies description. And this is only the gateway to the West!"

The expedition moved on at daybreak, following the north bank of the Platte. Setting a leisurely pace gave Wes and the others time for collecting. After supper he dictated to Emma the highlights he wanted noted in the journal that she would keep of the journey. Then he supervised and advised in the dissecting and mounting of small animals captured during the day, and the proper classification of beetles, butterflies, birds, snakes, minerals, and flowers. In another notebook, which he would fill with his labored scrawl, he began noting general geological observations of the changing country: from river bottom to rising dry-land plateau, the nature of the soil, the shape and course of the valley worn over eons of time by the Platte. When the evening light petered out, he rallied his crew around a campfire to sing. But the relaxation was brief. Even the Major retired early, his body weary from long hours in the saddle. No one escaped sore muscles and blisters.

On June 23 the party crossed the Bijou Basin fifty miles east of Denver. A fine drizzle limited visibility to a few miles. A few grumbled about damp clothing, but Wes cheered them: "It's a perfect day for collecting. The insects and birds aren't as active as usual."

Late that afternoon the sky began to clear as the gray rain clouds moved eastward. Suddenly the last wisps were blown away. In a blaze of red and gold sunlight Wes had his first, unforgettable sight of the massive thrust of the Rocky Mountains — pine-flanked, rock-ribbed, snowy peaks glowing. He stopped the caravan, stood in his stirrups, and cheered. Then he settled back again and slaked his long yearning for a sight of these mountains, gazing so steadily that his eyes watered.

He had an unexplainable tenuous feeling of having "come home." The mountains drew him like a powerful magnet. He could feel the actual pull in his breast. "What are we dallying here for?" he called out. "Let's go!" He rode off at a speed that left the others far behind. For a little while he wanted to be alone, out in front. It was a trait he would never lose as long as his legs and heart could carry him up mountains and down canyons.

By July the Major led the way into Denver, amazed to find it a town of 5,000 people with brick stores lining a business district. Well aware that good publicity would enhance the prestige of the little expedition, he presented his story to William

N. Byers, editor of *The Rocky Mountain News*. Byers published an extravagantly complimentary account, which was duly reprinted in the home papers. The museum directors were most gratified. The Powell families were relieved that, so far, Wes and Emma had not been scalped.

Editor Byers also gave the Major some advice that was to have far-reaching effects: "If you're interested in climbing Pike's Peak, contact my brother-in-law, Jack Sumner. He's an outfitter, and the best guide in Middle Park, Colorado. For your own welfare, don't go through the high country without an experienced guide." Byers chuckled. "If you got lost, it would be a whale of a story. But I don't want to have to organize a searching party to rescue you."

Climb Pike's Peak? "I hadn't seriously considered it," the Major murmured. Once Byers had suggested it, however, he couldn't get rid of the idea. He talked with Emma and shared the suggestion with the others. The tenderfeet were tremendously enthusiastic. "Let's do it!"

Before leaving Denver, the Major replenished supplies and shipped home boxes of specimens. Then he busied himself studying the routes to the peak. One was eighty miles over a well-worn road; the other, shorter but more difficult, led over the Rampart Range to Bergen's Park. "Which shall we take?"

The party voted for the more rugged trail because it promised better collecting.

It proved a tough initiation to mountain travel. Prairie-raised Wes Powell and his companions not only had to worry about the uphill tussle, but how to keep their footing going sidewise and down! Finally the summit was reached.

"It isn't a very big mountain," the Major admitted, "but isn't the view a popper?" To the south he saw the massive shoulders and cloud-crested apex of Pike's Peak; east, the shimmering plains; north, a gigantic parade of somber forests; further west, higher mountain ranges soared one behind the other.

There was scant time for sight-seeing. "The trouble with

climbing a mountain is that you can't stay on top." He led the descent. It meant digging in at the heels, chocking wheels, straining on ropes to brake the lumbering wagons, the Major sharing in the labor. All this was forgotten as soon as bedrolls were spread on fragrant pine boughs and he sniffed the pine-clean air.

Wes couldn't sleep. At last he had topped a mountain! Emma tried to calm him, but he kept saying, "This is only the beginning! Think what lies off to the west! Did you see all those mountains?" Suddenly he sat up, an auburn-haired, bright-eyed explorer swathed in a patchwork quilt. "I've got to see all of it, Emma, every secret, hidden inch of it. I can't stop now!"

His exhausted wife murmured sleepily, "You'll see it, darling, but please shush and go to sleep!"

The next day the horses and wagons moved on to Bergen's Park, a narrow, grassy meadow twenty miles long, flanked by high mountains, with sparkling creeks cascading down from icy springs high in the rocks.

It was a collector's paradise.

The Major's companions were ecstatic. In sun and rain, despite thunderstorms and a light snowfall, they scoured the meadow and slopes. The collections, in number and variety, grew beyond their wildest hopes. Each member had specific tasks: insects and plants to dry and press for shipping, animal skins to stretch, skeletons to sketch, fossils to extract, minerals to classify, the thousandfold tasks of a scientific field expedition. The Major still supervised all this, but now he began serious work in his own specialty, geology.

During morning, noon, and night stops he made geological maps of the region. These rough field sketches, refined later, consisted of side or front profile line drawings of Bergen Park, its slopes, creek drainages, and peaks. Additional lines showed where a creek had cut through a ridge of tilted beds of rock, which he identified as *igneous* — rocks solidified by cooling out of molten magma (liquid rock) such as the granites of the topmost peaks; or *sedimentary* — those formed by great pressure or

chemical cementation from sand, mud, or gravel such as limestone outcroppings; or *metamorphic* — those that eons before
were originally igneous or sedimentary but metamorphosed
(changed) due to heat, pressure, or water. He noted glacial
action, drew fracture lines to show where mountains had split,
one portion moving above, below, or to the side of its original
mass. Scalloped lines indicated where a portion of the earth's
crust had been squeezed together during the mountain-forming
Upper Cretaceous period, when the Rockies were pushed up
along with the general uplifting of the Western plateaus. Wes
knew this was also the age of the dinosaurs, so he sought their
fossil remains diligently, but fruitlessly, on this trip.

However crude his sketches were — unavoidably so when
drawn with the left hand — they gave a vivid impression of high
country, soaring peaks, tumbling water courses, and undulating
meadows. The Major scrambled up rocky slopes and roamed
far gathering as many samples of rocks, minerals, and crystals
as were to be found. Although he drove himself mercilessly, he
could not see, sketch, and collect half enough. He had forgotten
that he was a maimed man.

The sky was still dark the early hours of July 27 when preparations for the ascent of Pike's Peak began. There was no
chance of getting lost because the peak, higher than surrounding mountains, loomed above them. The Major, Emma, and six
others would make the try.

The Major laced his sturdy boots without help now. His
heavy trousers, wool shirt, and jacket were already weathered.
His pockets bulged with notebook, magnifying glass, rock
hammer, and binoculars. A battered hat completed his regalia.

Emma's husband might be casually attired, but not Emma.
Her neat, one-piece dress of waterproof material decorously
reached the top of her high-buttoned shoes. She wore a brimmed
hat secured with green veil and as many petticoats as practi-
cality and style deemed lady-like.

The climb was difficult. First on horseback, later on foot, the

Major led the way over boulders and twisted dead timber, across boggy places and precipitous ridges. Before midday he halted for a lunch of cold beef and crackers. The 9,000-foot altitude made him short of breath. By three o'clock, panting as much from excitement as exertion, he reached the 14,110-foot-high summit, the others at his heels.

At last he could look out over incredible distances. It was a dramatic eye-opener to a onetime prairie lad, who had never ventured above timber line. "We haven't climbed just to see the scenery," he said after a moment. He and the others scurried around, studying the stunted evergreens, lichens, and insects and gathering specimens.

Wholly absorbed, the Major lingered too long. With a bitter wind and swift-approaching darkness catching him unawares, it was impossible to escape or hurry. He led the way downward, groping, testing, sliding. "Timber line!" he shouted hours later. "Let's have a fire and a rest and go on at daybreak."

By noon all were back at the campsite, the Major high-strung, exulting over the success, happy to have specimens from the summit. Few museums could boast that! Emma was proud to be the first woman to scale Pike's Peak.

After a rest the Major made contact with Jack Sumner.

The two, the slight professor and the tall, rangy blue-eyed mountain man, eyed each other. The Major survived the scalpeling look because he had the indefinable stamp of the outdoorsman. Not so the others. One scathing glance from the guide reduced them to the status of tenderfeet. Many years later, in writing of his long association with the Major on this and other explorations, Jack Sumner described this first group as "about as fit for roughing it as Hades is for a Powder house." Cool, a crack shot, Sumner was used to handling dudes, even science-minded crazy ones who went galloping all over creation for butterflies and rocks.

He led the Major through the mountains into South Park, another paradise. One night by the campfire he mentioned, "Got a little something I've always been meanin' to do. So far, no one has discovered the source of the South Platte River. It's up thar. How about you 'n me scoutin' around for a day or two?"

The Major was like a beagle scenting a fox. He told his party to catch up on their laboratory work while he and Sumner were away.

Before leaving, the Major consulted his maps. Unlike the mountain man, who would rely solely on his sense of direction and observation of creek flow, Wes used science to help him pinpoint the general area from which the headwaters must issue. Sumner scoffed, but two days later, after a few false leads, they came upon a remote, snow-fed lake that Wes had traced upward and could substantiate as the true source of the South Platte.

His chest expanded at least three inches as he realized he had a "first" to his credit. However small, it was his discovery, and whetted his appetite to add more to this modest laurel.

After he reunited with his party the journey resumed. The Major completed his geological observations and sketch of South Park. Meanwhile new items were being gathered by his cohorts: skins of bear, elk, and wolverine. Not until snow threatened to trap them on a high pass did the Major call a halt. The expedition returned to Denver where all but the Powells departed for the East. Emma took care of the details, while the Major scurried around gathering more mineral specimens, visiting mines underground, and watching the processing of ores.

It was September now, that brief golden period when turquoise skies were cloudless over the valleys and mosquitoes and deer flies no longer troublesome.

The Major suggested, "Why hurry home? Jack Sumner has proposed a thrilling new project for next summer: exploring the approaches to the Grand River, then tracing its headwaters to its junction with the mighty Colorado? Why don't we see if it's plausible?"

The Major, Emma, and Sumner spent two months examining

the more easily accessible canyons along the Grand River. Soon the next summer's project was a foregone conclusion. The Major was confident that ingenuity (and his skill as a politician) would provide the means. "I'll have to put practically all of my salary toward the expenses," he warned Emma. As usual, she was agreeable.

By November 1 the Powells, bronzed, seasoned mountain travelers, impatient for their next adventure, returned to Denver. After storing their equipment and shipping more boxes home, they said farewell to Sumner. The Major fattened his lean purse with a whirlwind spate of writing newspaper articles and making speeches. On November 6, 1867, he and Emma left by stage for Illinois.

As they bumped and rocked in the stagecoach, Wes had time to think about the future. Sumner and Emma saw no further than exploring the Grand. He saw it as the next step in a supreme adventure. Unwittingly, Jack Sumner had suggested the boldest plan of all to him — explore and map the mile-deep Grand Canyon of the Colorado. It was a glorious dream of Sumner, though he admitted, "No man has ever done it. The few who tried died in the attempt."

It was the ultimate in exploration. Memory served Wes as he recalled Dr. Mather's prediction that someday someone would conquer the untamed giant, the mighty Colorado, still the last unknown portion of America twenty-four years later.

At last John Wesley Powell had found his great goal, his all-absorbing purpose. "I never in my life felt so right about anything," he told himself. "Now I know what I want in life. I want to be an explorer and a geologist. I'm through dibble-dabbling around. I'm going to explore that canyon, and I won't give up until I've succeeded or died in the effort."

The Major drove toward that goal with furious intensity. Everything — every breath, every penny, every hour spent collecting, or circumventing barriers, all his creative thinking — was geared toward one of the most stupendous explorations in history. "First the Grand," he planned, naming a river that many considered the Upper Colorado. Then he would keep on going down, down, through the canyon of the Great Unknown.

It was too soon to tell Emma or his closest friends. He would not hint of the grand plan to the newspapers. But from this moment on, Major Powell used science and sheer grit to tear off the veil of mystery shrouding a vast portion of his beloved country. He promised himself, "I'm going to have the best adventure of my life!"

CHAPTER TEN

FIRST ATOP LONG'S PEAK

"Astonishing! Such variety! Major, your collections will make ours the most outstanding museum of natural history in the Midwest." The directors of the Illinois State Natural History Society were thrilled when the Major presented them with a catalogued, mounted display of nine hundred birds, hundreds of plants, thousands of insects, and a significant showing of minerals.

An ordinary man would have been content to spend years lecturing on the collection, riding the same old trail. Not John Wesley Powell. Two weeks later he rocked the directors back on their heels: "I want you to underwrite funds for a second, more ambitious expedition."

"Where?"

"I want to be the first to climb Long's Peak in Colorado. I surveyed the approaches to it, and I think I know how it can be done."

The chairman of the board pointed out, "This means even greater prestige for us if the Major succeeds."

"I'll succeed," he assured them. He appeared confident but nervous. Actually it wasn't nerves. He was already champing at the bit to be on his way to Long's Peak.

For months he busied himself with his classes, lectures, field trips. Emma served as his amanuensis and was hard put to keep up with his lively correspondence with fellow scientists. He made another trip to Washington to wangle rations, transportation, the loan of instruments, and more money.

Once more the Major chose his personnel from amateur rather than highly trained scientists, friends, and relatives. Emma, the Major's sister Nell, her husband, congenial Harry Thompson, and the much-improved Walter were included: twenty-one all told, with a few student assistants, each paying his own expenses.

On June 29, 1868, the Major helped tack a huge banner onto the baggage car that would transport their equipment and supplies from Chicago to Cheyenne, Wyoming. The black letters read COLORADO SCIENTIFIC EXPLORING EXPEDITION.

"Looks good, doesn't it?" he decided, a warm feeling reddening his cheeks. "We may be a scrimpy outfit, but we have an imposing title."

Cheyenne was a jolt. Even the Major gaped at the crude stores with false two-story fronts, the bat-winged doors of the saloons, the raucous conduct of the cowboys. Across the railroad tracks a band of wild horses kicked up the dust. The ground was littered with prairie-dog warrens.

The Major kept his group at the depot until their duffel was loaded onto breachy horses and mules. He was glad to mount his horse and lead the way toward Denver, climbing steadily into the high country. Everyone swallowed dust, fought fleas, was bucked into the sagebrush, cooked over smoking campfires, which he jovially referred to as the initiation period. "The mosquitoes are worse than I ever saw them," he wrote in his diary. Soon he had recovered from aching muscles, sunburn, saddle sores, and cactus barbs. His round nose was as red as an apple.

The Major hurried through Denver. "We've seen it." He went on to Clear Creek, on through Bear Creek Canyon and west to

Empire City. Here William N. Byers, the editor of *The Rocky Mountain News*, joined the expedition. Byers was an ardent sportsman, sharing Powell's enthusiasm for conquering Long's Peak. He wasn't too keen on spending more than a week, as the Major insisted, in the cradle of Berthoud Pass — 11,314 feet high — at a time when the alpine flowers were most dazzling. Every hour, every mile here offered something new for each individual's specialty.

"There are no half-way measures about the weather," the Major wrote by firelight as he perched on a sack of beans. "We are buffeted by wind, skidding temperatures, even snow. The specimens surpass our fondest expectations."

On sunny days he strode at a high lope from dawn to dark, studying and sketching the high country's geological formations, and he still found time to keep his finger on each member's progress.

Byers' contribution was of a more practical nature. He kept the camp larder supplied with elk, venison, wild fowl, and trout.

The Major took his time moving down from the pass into Middle Park and camped at Hot Sulphur Springs.

"Another collector's paradise!" he exclaimed, relentlessly urging his associates to increase their labors. Some grumbled, but after a few encouraging words from their leader, they put forth the extra effort. One of the student assistants, a serious-minded Quaker lad named Sam Garman, who worshiped Powell because of his drive and brilliance, said ruefully, "The Major works harder than any of us. We don't dare complain out loud."

Jack Sumner joined them there. The greenhorns gawked at the tough mountain man. Once more, when he flicked a glance at their gear, they curdled down to "dude" level. But Sumner was content; he had the Major and his own brother-in-law for company.

"How many are going up Long's Peak?" he asked.

Seven voted to try. Emma stayed behind with Nell. The

Major, Sumner, Walter, Byers, and the three students, Sam
Garman, L. W. Keplinger, and Ned Farrell, left Grand Lake on
August 20. Each man was mounted, armed with pistol and rifle,
and led a pack mule containing ten days' rations and scientific
instruments. The first night the Major called a halt at timber
line. The next morning, before the others were stirring, he was
up making biscuits in honor of the occasion.

"I didn't count on carrying lead weights to the summit,"
Byers joked.

"How can you tell Wes' biscuits from the rocks?" Walter
asked.

His brother had an answer. "Nothing else stays with you
longer than my biscuits."

As soon as each had fixed his small back pack, the Major led
the final ascent. The first few tries were failures. In spite of
being slightly off-balance because of the loss of his arm, he did
not balk at knife-edged ridges. While climbing, each man had
his eyes on the ground, locating a safe foot- or handhold. When
the Major stopped to get his breath and looked around, he
found that the world dropped away several thousand feet beneath him. He squeezed his eyes shut, shivered, clung desperately to the rocks. After that he didn't look around any more
than was absolutely necessary.

Jack Sumner was having a fine time watching the greenhorns
sweat out the dizzying heights. At one bad place the Major
unashamedly got down on his knees and crept along, balancing
on his good arm. The mountain man meant to brazen it out
standing up; but when he slipped and almost fell over the edge
of the precipice, he got down and *cooned* it, like the Major.

Try as he might, Powell could not find the way to the top.
Keplinger, sliding and clawing along the northwest corner of
the Notch, was successful. He reported his find. Wes gladly
followed Keplinger, asking no quarter for his one-armed strug-
gles. When he needed assistance, he asked for it. The seven

crept the final seven hundred feet on hands and knees. Suddenly the Major realized that the rocks no longer pitched upward before his face. He looked around, then jumped to his feet. "Glory to God!" he shouted. "We made it!" The bitter wind tore the words from his lips.

The view almost knocked him over. The others pounded each other's shoulders and pointed in every direction. The Major and Sumner soon concentrated their attention on the country to the west. The quiet, knowing glances they exchanged meant, "There it is. That's where we're going, what we have to conquer. God grant we live to do it!" The country looked as if it had been tossed and beaten and hacked with a gigantic knife.

On that windy knob of granite, where no man had stood before, Major John Wesley Powell raised the American flag on August 23, 1868. The students built a cairn of stones to support the pole.

Tearing a sheet from his notebook, he wrote the date and hour and then signed his name, *Major John Wesley Powell, Leader, Colorado Scientific Exploring Expedition.* Underneath Jack Sumner, William N. Byers, Walter Powell, L. W. Keplinger, Sam Garman, and Ned Farrell added their names. When Keplinger had finished taking barometric readings and the temperatures, this information was included, the paper rolled and cached in a small baking-powder can, which the Major had brought along for just such an occasion.

Keplinger joked, "How about putting one of your biscuits in the can as a memento?"

The Major frowned on such frivolity. "This is a solemn occasion. Let's get on with our scientific observations and collecting." Science must be served with dignity, first, last, always. The can was buried in the cairn without further ceremony.

Where his companions were jubilant, John Wesley Powell was overcome with the sobering aspect of what lay ahead of him. He was already thinking of the future. It seemed that once he accomplished something, he immediately lost interest in it, save for the aspects or experience that paved the way for another project. He looked down upon Middle Park, beyond it to the Gore Range, past the Rabbit Ears, toward the unexplored Canyon of the Colorado. He vowed that even though it cost him his life, his destiny lay westward in the great Unknown.

CHAPTER ELEVEN

EXPLORING THE GRAND

The Major and his party returned to Grand Lake, supposedly to rest from the grueling climb. Twenty-four hours later he was supervising the packing of bales of specimens, which he shipped East by mule train over Berthoud Pass to Denver and far-off Illinois.

Before leaving with the pack train, Editor Byers promised, "You'll be a celebrity after I get through publicizing our ascent."

Since Middle Park was a paradise for scientists as well as sportsmen, the Major lingered there to complete his field maps. Word came to him that one of the most eminent newspapermen in the country was camped nearby. Samuel Bowles of the Springfield (Massachusetts) *Republican* was one of a number of editors who rushed West after the Civil War to report on its resources and opportunities. He was happy to give further publicity to Powell's accomplishments and the expedition's scientific work. The Major, deciding to give Bowles something of an editorial scoop, told him about his next project.

"The great and final object of the expedition," Bowles wrote, "is to explore the Upper Colorado River and solve the mysteries of its three-hundred-mile canyon . . . The maps from Washington, that put down only what is absolutely, scientifically known, leave a great blank space here of three hundred to five hundred miles long, and one hundred to two hundred miles broad. Is any other nation so ignorant of itself?"

His column, reprinted in Midwestern papers, was seen by Wes' family. "Explore the Upper Colorado!" they exclaimed. "That's the first we've heard of it."

"We didn't say he could do that," a fussy director of the museum objected. "I move that we write the Major to come home at once."

"Why bother?" another said resignedly. "By the time he gets the letter, he will have done it."

The Major finished his geological observations for the area and gave the rough sketches to Harry Thompson for delivery to the Natural History Society. Thompson had taken a fancy to mapping, and proved uncommonly skilled. "Major, how about letting me save you a lot of time by refining these sketches before I present them to the directors?"

Wes was agreeable. "Go ahead, but be sure you take credit for the drawing." Thus Harry Thompson took the first big step toward becoming one of the most skilled, artist-mapmakers of his generation.

Shortly after, the Major bade farewell to Harry and Nell and some of the original personnel of the expedition. "It's been a successful summer," he evaluated it modestly.

Meanwhile Jack Sumner had been scouting around and reported that a village of Ute Indians were camped nearby. The Major was delighted, for he had been asked by Professor Joseph Henry, secretary of the Smithsonian Institution, "to gather as much information as possible on the Indians of the west." Interested in Indians ever since he had dug in his first burial ground with George Crookham, Wes was anxious to comply, but wished he didn't have to spend precious time on routine tasks when something new beckoned him. "Could you and Walter superintend the packing?" he asked Emma.

She was agreeable. So was Walter, sturdy now, finding mountain travel much to his liking. Too moody and often surly, except with his family, to be popular, Walter was nonetheless a valuable asset to any frontier party.

Fortunately Sumner knew enough Ute words to present the Major to the chief, and he served as interpreter while Wes jotted down a partial vocabulary. The visit was far too brief. "I hope we will meet more Utes in the back country," he said.

"You will," Sumner answered wryly, "but I can't swear how sociable they will be."

On their return to camp, they found that Emma and Walter had done an excellent job of packing. All Wes needed to do was mount his horse. He and Sumner led the way through Cedar Canyon on the Park Range, past the Rabbit Ears with the remaining members of the expedition: five students, two scientists, Emma, Walter, and a motley crew of laborers. They camped on steep slopes, in heavy timber, beside creeks, in meadows where the sun-ripened grass was knee-high. They probed deeper into the White River primitive area. Aspen flamed on the pine-flanked ridges. Frost-burnished shrubs glowed along the creek bottoms. At times the sky was shadowed with flying wedges of southbound water fowl. Elk shattered the stillness with their massive, blasting rutting calls.

"I admit that getting up in the morning is a bit of a chore," the Major said one morning, breathing on his frosted fingers. Tents and blankets were rimed with frost. Emma was blue, but still game. The others cursed the numbing cold under their breath.

In a snug valley now known as Powell Park, or Powell Bottoms, near the modern town of Meeker, Colorado, the Major decided, "We'll make our winter camp here." After helping build cabins the last two weeks in October, 1868, he told Emma, "I want to move around the country a bit before we're snowbound. Could you and Walter — "

She and Walter would see that the wild hay was cut for forage, an immense woodpile stocked, game butchered, and the carcasses hung in the shed. Snow was already falling. Emma ordered shelving, tables, and other simple furniture built for the cabin she and Wes would use. "Everything must be done to accommodate the Major," she kept saying when the men grumbled over the extra work.

Meanwhile Wes and Jack Sumner gallivanted up and down the Grand, the weather no threat to them. The Major didn't mind a cold saddle, or burrowing under blankets with only brush to keep off the snow. "I'm mapping the heretofore un-mapped. I'm serving science." He wasn't just content. "My cup runneth over," he said prayerfully. The Grand wasn't as tough a nut to crack as he had been told. He sketched mesas dark with juniper and scrub pine, traced the cottonwood and willow-bordered courses of the tributary creeks. He built fires to thaw the ground so he could study the soil. He mapped the confusion of lateral gulches. "Wonderful, wonderful," he sang out time and time again. "I'm getting the feel of the country."

Sumner snorted. He was getting the feel all right. The Major had about run the legs off him.

They pushed on to the Green River and teetered briefly on the edge of its precipitous, flaming red rock canyon. "We'll be back here next summer with our Colorado River expedition. Now that I've seen the Green, it holds no terrors for me. Boats are the answer to our problem."

When he and his companion returned to camp, Wes was astounded at all that had been accomplished. "You've done wonders!" he complimented his men and Emma. They appreciated the compliment. He was a popular leader because of this very consideration for the supreme efforts others put forth.

One of the camptenders spoke out. "Major, we ain't got enough staple supplies to last a full crew the winter. Some of us would just as soon go out to the railhead, if you'll take us."

Despite the fact that it was November, the Major led them northward across one hundred and seventy-five miles of storm-wracked plateau country to the nearest railroad at Green River Crossing, Wyoming. Sumner and O. G. Howland, a former printer-turned-guide, accompanied him so he need not return alone.

"Let's not retrace our path," the Major suggested when they had waved good-by to their friends. The fact that their path was long since swept clean with wind and fresh snow was immaterial. He didn't like to back-track. "I'd like to swing around the east of the Uintahs. They're the only mountains in the West that run east and west."

"You're the boss," Howland agreed. He felt that only scientists and fools would plan such a trip in mid-winter, but he would follow the Major anywhere.

Slowly, arduously, the three worked around the base of the Uintahs.

"Too bad you weren't born a generation earlier," Sumner told Powell as they huddled over a small fire, waiting for the can of tea to boil. "You'd have given Jim Bridger and Jed Smith a fair chase." With a trace of exasperation he exclaimed, "Don't you mind being cold? Or being on short rations? You never say anything. Don't you worry about what might happen? It would be only normal if you did."

The Major blinked. "I guess I like my creature comforts as much as any man . . . Yes, I dislike being cold and hungry. But when I'm exploring, discomfort just doesn't register with me. I'm so absorbed in my work, nothing else gets through to me." Then he added, "No, I don't worry about what might happen. I just keep plugging ahead and leave my life in God's hands."

The Major almost moved ahead too fast. Within sight of home camp he was striding through the aspen, ignoring the underbrush that tripped him. Suddenly he heard a loud thrashing not thirty feet away. He halted, with Howland and Sumner almost plowing into him. A grizzly showed its head, then reared its full terrifying height. Another bear appeared, snarling frightfully.

The Major tore off his mitten with his teeth. He hefted his rifle, pulled back the safety lock with his thumb, and fired. As he dropped the barrel between his knees, dug for another cartridge, rammed it home, and raised to fire again, his companions' guns barked, almost shattering his eardrums. He fired again and watched his target crumple. After a second round from Sumner, the other grizzly fell at his feet.

"Now you're a bona-fide mountain man," Sumner shouted, banging Wes on the back with his fists.

Reaction gripped the Major. He almost whinnied, he was so relieved. "This is one tale I'll be grateful to be able to tell!"

Knowing the carcasses would soon freeze in the frigid temperature, he put down his rifle and took out his hunting knife. "What a magnificent specimen!" he crowed, the scientist in him coming to the fore.

"These hides will come in handy when it's fifty below," Howland remarked, getting on with the skinning.

"It's the bear fat that interests me most," the Major admitted, puffing as he helped Howland. "After it's rendered out, think of all the lamp oil we will have."

Sumner and Howland exchanged glances. The Major had killed a grizzly. But apparently what mattered most to him was that there would be plenty of lamp oil for the long winter nights when he would be writing his scientific reports. "What a guy!" Sumner said under his breath.

That winter would not be a time for huddling close to the fireplace. Ute Indians appeared, begging food. The Major returned to their camp and spent some time visiting with Chief Douglas and his people. It never occurred to him to go armed or to ask for a protective escort. Emma accompanied him a number of times to sketch the braves and squaws, learn their language, and record their vocabulary.

The Major worked out a fair exchange. He had noticed that the Utes, having no firearms, still hunted with bow and arrow. No wonder winter was a lean time for them. He signified, through finger talk and his growing command of their language, that if they would cooperate with his studies, his hunters would furnish plenty of meat.

Emma endured the fleas, the lice, the smells (even in winter), and the not-to-be-guessed-at contents of stew simmering in an ancient kettle, but could not free herself of prejudice. "I think I'm a good Christian," she remarked to Wes one night as they huddled under bearskins with their feet toward the fire, "but I can't see these Utes as you do. You treat them as if they were your equal. To me, they're little better than animals."

Drawing deep on his religious convictions, Wes answered firmly, "In the sight of God, all men are equal, Emma."

This attitude was the key to John Wesley Powell's astounding success with the primitive tribes of the canyon country. He did not try to make them change their religion or their way of life. Because of this they talked freely to him, and he was able to record volumes on their customs, myths, and languages.

He was still following in the pattern of George Crookham. The more he knew these Utes and other unspoiled tribes as yet uncorrupted by white influence, the more he respected them. His systematic collections of beadwork, buckskin leggings, basketwork, pottery and utensils, and his written recordings of their vocabularies were a revelation to the Smithsonian Institution.

Later, every time a box of field notes and handcraft articles arrived from Powell, Professor Henry would exclaim, "Another gold mine! The man is a genius! Does he realize what a tremendous service he is doing for his country in gathering this information? If he keeps this up, the Smithsonian will be one of the world centers of ethnological research!"

Without realizing it just yet, the Major was dividing his intensive loyalty to geology. In time he would become one of the nation's experts on the origins, characteristics, and physical and linguistic classifications of the Indians of the West.

In spite of the work indoors and out, the studies, drawings, mapmaking, the daily drudgery of keeping warm and well fed in the winter wilderness, there was time for friction to develop between members of his party. The men, too much in one another's company, too closely confined in the small cabins, became irritable. Only on one thing were they agreed — all were fed up with Emma.

"If that-there female don't stop bossin' me around," one of the camptenders threatened, "I'll plumb forgit she's a woman and treat her like a squaw!"

Another volunteered, "Nag, nag, nag, nag! 'Cut wood, Charlie. Carry out the slops, Charlie. Wash your socks. Take a bath.'" The man exploded, "Take a bath? What in? A tin cup? Scrub my back with icicles?" He mimicked Emma savagely, "'I suggest you read this book of poems, Mr. So-and-So. It will improve your mind.'" The man spat into the fireplace. "If there's anything I can't abide, it's a bossy woman."

When the grumbling amounted to rebellion, the Major had to tear himself from his absorption in his studies to negotiate a peace. However much the men admired Emma's fortitude and cheerfulness, they would not tolerate one more order from her. "Your lady says you and she is joint commanders here," the spokesman complained, breathing heavily. "That ain't what we understood last fall. We're willin' to take orders from you, Major, and Jack Sumner here, but nobody else. The lady leaves us be, or we walk out!"

Wes was aghast. Apparently he had let Emma take over too many things so that he could be free to study. He knew she was a strong-minded woman, but he adored her. If she had become bossy, it was only to make things easier for him. "I'll tend to it," he promised the men.

Back at the cabin, he said, "My dear, it looks as though we must — er," he cleared his throat and paused. He couldn't bear to hurt Emma's feelings. "We must make certain adjustments," he said vaguely.

Emma waited to have her dear Wes tell her what he wanted done.

"What I mean is . . . After this, perhaps you'd better —— "

"Yes, dear?" Emma had never known him to be so vacillating. Was he getting run-down from all this wilderness exploration?

Wes mopped his forehead. He was perspiring freely. "It's hot in here. Hot in the bunkhouse too. I've — I've just come from there." How in heaven, he wondered frantically, could he . . . Suddenly he had an inspiration. "You know, dear, when men are cooped up in small quarters and can't work off their energies outside, they get cabin fever. Sometimes they get violent."

"Yes, I know."

"Our boys are the best," he went on, feeling his way in this delicate situation, "but they're — they've reached — well, they're on edge! From now on, I'll feel a lot better if you just stay in our cabin and tend to your own chores. Let me deal with the men. For your sake," he stressed.

"Of course, dear, if that's your wish." Emma had taken to "managing" like a duck to water. But she was grateful to have a husband who would protect her.

Wes kissed her. "You're the most wonderful wife in the world. You're my right arm, my helpmate, my everything! But from now on, let me give the orders, eh, darling? We can't afford trouble in so remote a camp."

Emma had heard plenty about men and women going crazy with cabin fever. Horrors, what if the crew went wild and set fire to the camp! Nothing must happen to harm her Wes' precious reports and maps. She returned his embrace. "I'll do just as you say."

The Major relaxed. He slipped out of his heavy jacket and sank into a chair by the cheery fireplace. He felt as if he had just weathered a desperate crisis. Then he laughed deep inside himself. "Handling a woman can be as touch-and-go as meeting a grizzly," he realized with new-found wisdom.

Fortunately, spring was in the offing. The situation cleared
when he took the malcontents on a rugged reconnaissance of
the Grand River canyon, then over to the White River again,
and its junction with the Green. By April the Major was ready
to break camp. The map in his mind was clear. All that remained to be done was design boats for the rough water, make
the usual contacts in Washington, and find sponsors to underwrite the expense.

Once more ingenuity served him well. A thousand problems
were overcome, the doubting Thomases mowed down by his
overpowering confidence. On May 23, 1869, boats, personnel,
supplies, leader — all were ready for the journey into the Unknown.

CHAPTER TWELVE

THE CONQUEST OF
THE COLORADO

At Green River Crossing, Wyoming, on May 24, 1869, three specially designed *rowboats*, twenty-one feet long and sturdily built with airtight compartments, pulled on their mooring lines like young broncs fighting headstalls. The stubborn current of the Green tugged at them, rocking the lighter sixteen-foot pine pilot boat, christened the *Emma Dean.*

Major John Wesley Powell inspected his small flotilla. Ten months' rations and all the impedimenta of a scientific expedition were neatly stored among the three larger boats. Every kind of emergency had been anticipated. And Emma was comfortably housed with her parents in Detroit.

He stepped the length of the pilot boat, its jaunty flag snapping in the morning breeze. As his hand touched the long rear sweep, he felt it throbbing against the relentless current. The Green was an ominous river at all times, even here on a quiet stretch.

Shading his eyes with his left hand, the Major looked beyond the river's barren banks to the weirdly eroded tan and brown buttes soaring from the parched Badlands. It was lonely, desolate country. Ahead lay 1,500 miles of unknown canyon travail, with not one outpost along its course. "What a geologist's para-

103

dise!" he thought happily. "None of it mapped beyond here, all mine to discover."

Jack Sumner sauntered up, loose-limbed, his light blue eyes blazing with excitement. "This day has been a long time coming, Major!" he said. The mountain man was one of the oarsmen for the Major's pilot boat, along with Bill Dunn, another crony whose dirty buckskins and shoulder-length black hair belied his intelligence. Two excursions with the Major had welded Sumner's respect for his leader into a rock-firm faith that he would succeed where others had failed.

The Major grinned and extended his hand. "We're going to make it, Jack."

Sumner offered his left hand easily. "You bet we are!"

Young George Bradley joined them. His was a new face. The Major had petitioned his release from frontier army service because he was a skilled boatman and an amateur geologist. Bradley was put in charge of the *Kitty Clyde's Sister,* along with Walter Powell.

"Where's Andy?" the Major asked, referring to the youngest member, an eighteen-year-old Scottish lad who had drifted into Green River and had been hired when he proved to be both competent and good-natured. Knowing that some of his crew like Sumner, Bradley, and Walter were men of few words and often of dour disposition, the Major felt that Andy's sunny disposition, his jokes and laughter, would be a welcome asset.

"Andy is still at Jake's Eatery stuffing himself with ham and eggs and apple pie," Bradley answered. "He says he's going to put down enough to last him forty days. He figures it will take Billy Hawkins that long to learn to cook."

"I heard you!" Hawkins protested as he came up. "Quit insultin' my chow. You ain't et any of it yit, so how come you an' Andy talk that way?" He chuckled. "Here come the rest of 'em, full as ticks. Bet they swamp the boats."

O. G. Howland, the bear-killer of last year, and his brother

Seneca called, "What are we waiting for?" and took their places in the *No-Name*. "Come on, Frank, get the dust off your boots."

Frank Goodman was an English gentleman-hunter in search of thrills. He had just happened to be passing through Green River, heard about the expedition, and agreed to pay his expenses if taken along. Wes had let the crew decide. They had voted aye, and the Major was secretly glad to have another able-bodied man on the roster. "Ahoy the Col-or-ah-dooo!" Goodman cheered. "Let's be off!"

"Ready?" the Major called out. He took one last look around before departure. He had trained each man beforehand in his separate duties, flag signals, and scientific work. They were all rugged, experienced in wilderness survival, wary of the river opponent, and absolutely fearless.

"Shove off!" he ordered, waving good-by to the few curious townspeople who had gathered around the boats.

Lines were hauled aboard. The oars cut the muddy, swirling water. The sun blazed down as the current grabbed, pushing hard on the four boats and the ten men. In a few minutes they had swung around a bend and were out of sight.

As they camped the first night in a cottonwood grove near the water, Billy Hawkins had trouble cooking his first meal "on the road," as he called it.

"Would it help if I made the biscuits?" the Major suggested.

"Don't let him do it," Walter pleaded.

Sumner said owlishly, "Major, I'll follow you to the ends of the earth and no questions asked. But I be danged if I'll eat any more of your biscuits!"

"All right," Wes said, laughing. "I'll set up the drawing board and get on with the mapping." He planned, at the end of each day, to make a geological sketch of the river banks and surrounding plateau. He would then add the scientific observations of depth, stream flow, barometric pressure, temperature, and mileage computed by Bradley and Walter. He had assigned the mapping of the river's meandering course to O. G. Howland.

Wes' intensive studies in geology had taught him that the eroded tableland back from the water and the rocks exposed in the low bluffs were of the Mesozoic era, the fourth of the five great eras in geologic time. But his great hope was to see that rarest of sights, Archeozoic rocks, the very oldest, exposed in the bed or walls of the Grand Canyon of the Colorado.

He sketched absorbedly until he heard Billy Hawkins yell in true bullwhacker fashion, "Plun-der! Go fur it, boys!"

"Go fur it!" Andy Hall shouted. "Boys, here's where we git it! Belly-aches, ahoy!"

Laughing, the men grabbed their tin plates and served themselves. The biscuits had been baked in a Dutch oven, a cast-iron skillet on short legs with a turned-up lid to hold hot coals. They were leathery and scorched, but appetizing when Hawkins ladled sizzling bacon fat over them.

"The beans take some chewing," Billy apologized.

"So do the dried apples," Dunn remarked, crunching them in his teeth.

"Hey, Billy, is this sugar or sand in the coffee?"

"Coffee!" Seneca Howland joshed. "It's strong enough to make a man rear right up on his heels and howl!"

Nevertheless there was not a scrap of food left. Later the men relaxed around the campfire. "The first ten miles were easy," Sumner said. The men nodded. Only two had suffered a wetting. But already they were learning the danger of running aground on a sand bar, or spinning in unsuspected eddies, of breaking an oar on a submerged rock.

"She's a lethal river every dang minute!" the elder Howland commented.

"Right-o!" Goodman agreed.

The next morning the Major had his men under way by daybreak. Before midday the bluffs loomed higher. The country was more broken up with cliffs and buttes. Even during a drenching rain, with the men pulling hard on the oars, the Major stood spraddle-legged in the middle of the *Emma Dean.* Occasionally he hauled a notebook from his pocket and, steadying it against his thigh with the stump of the right arm, scrawled various observations. At dusk he ordered the camp made near the water. Jack Sumner spotted a mountain sheep on a cliff behind them, and brought it down. The steaks were delicious, in spite of Billy's charring them. A chill wind kept all close to the fire and rolled in their blankets. "All quite merry," the Major noted in his journal for that night.

He had ordered astronomic observations made every fifty miles, and three times each day the altitude above sea level was computed from the river's edge with the aid of scientific instruments loaned by the Smithsonian. By using the water level as an ever-falling baseline, the Major and Bradley were able to compute the height of the canyon walls with surveying instruments. Both studied the rock strata exposed, and sketched geological sections of the countryside.

The Major never rested from daylight to dark. He wigwagged flag signals from the pilot boat and supervised the camp work. He scrambled up the steepening bluffs in order to study the area back from the river, and when darkness forced his return to camp, he busied himself with his notebooks. The others did the odd jobs of mending clothes and gear, and redistributing the loads so that the boats handled better. When they were all bedded down around the dying campfire, the Major usually suggested, "How about a song or two?" Walter's fine baritone voice added much to the crew's gravelly singing.

The second and third days were much like the first. There was no real canyon yet. The river ran smooth and swift. Sumner bagged a goose for supper, "and don't cook the life out of it," he warned Billy.

On May 26, after supper, the Major said, "Let's climb to the rim."

"I say, Major, haven't you had enough exercise for one day?" Goodman queried.

"Last one to the top scours the skillet!" Andy hollered and started climbing. The men worked their way up a cut worn in sloping, eroded benches by spring run-off. The Major pointed out from the rim. "That snug little valley to the south is Henry's Fork, a famed trapper rendezvous," he said. "Now look beyond. See where the river splits those red cliffs?"

Andy Hall's breath quickened. "Is that where the fast water starts?"

Walter grunted. "That's where trouble begins." When he was overly tired, Walter was surly, but the men understood his condition and ignored his remarks.

Goodman had glimpsed steeper canyons, so he said, though none with walls of flaming red rock. "Might be a bit of fun there," he added condescendingly. His opinion was received in silence, for his popularity had worn thin already. He treated some of the crew like servants, and dodged his share of the camp duties.

Although the men were anxious to test the boats on the white water, or rapids, the Major held them three days at the "gate" of the gorge while he made scientific observations. The cliffs overshadowing the Green River were now 1,200 feet high. His map showed the notched Wasatch Mountains on the west and the barren Wyoming plateau northward to the Wind River Mountains.

On the fourth day, while the crew broke camp, he put his thoughts on paper. "This morning we are ready to enter the mysterious cañon and start with some anxiety. The old mountaineers tell us that it cannot be run; the Indians say 'Water heap catch 'em,' but all are eager for the trial and off we go."

At the gateway the walls closed in suddenly, the water plunging swiftly among great rocks. The Major stood on his boat deck, signaling the passage. There were tense moments as the boats reached the swift current. They threaded the narrow passage with exhilirating velocity, mounting the high waves whose foaming crests dashed over them, then plunging into troughs, until they reached the quiet water below. A feeling of great relief came over them as they realized that their first rapid had been run.

As the boats glided into the quieter water, the Major cheered. The men answered with their own jubilant shouts. He wig-wagged them to shore for a cold lunch of biscuits and dried fruit.

"What's that roaring I hear downriver?" Andy asked his leader, already as disheveled as his companions. All were whiskered, their clothing fading from constant wetting and drying.

"More white water," the Major answered. "We're sure of a ducking. Let's everybody remove shoes and jackets."

Here the river swung to the left and carved a horseshoe-shaped canyon. Beyond this the boats slipped past a grassy park walled in by vertical cliffs, the river mirroring the towering cream and red rocks. With his flag the Major drew everyone's attention to a great dome, its face riddled with swallow's nests. Andy shouted, "It looks like Swiss cheese!" The Major later named it Beehive Point. Ahead was still another breathtakingly beautiful canyon, which he named for the blue kingfishers flocking there.

The next day Sumner and Dunn put the pilot boat through a rapid at tremendous speed. The Major had fixed footholds for himself and rode the pitching deck like a cowboy busting a bronc. When they faced a rapid too dangerous to run, he flagged them to the shore.

"Portage!" he called out.

"Aw, Major, we kin make it," Andy insisted.

"Sorry, we can't afford to lose a boat."

The crew sweated and toiled, letting the boats down foot by foot by means of one hundred and thirty foot ropes. The Major pulled his share of the load with the rope singeing burns on his hand as it whipped through his grasp. The others complained about having their arms almost wrenched from the sockets.

Camp that night was at the foot of a steep slope covered with pine trees. "As the twilight deepens," the Major wrote, "the rocks grow dark and somber; the threatening roar of the water is loud and constant, and I lie awake with thoughts of the morrow and the cañons to come."

He noted that the red sandstone cliffs now soared 2,500 feet above water level. "The canyon is getting steeper mile by mile, the water more dangerous, the surrounding country more desolate and remote." But he was far from depressed. In his watertight case were sheet after sheet of brand-new maps. Fatigue, discomfort, sunburn, plagues of mosquitoes — nothing dimmed the joy of his accomplishments.

On June 1 the boats raced through a very narrow slot which the Utes had described to the Major: "Rocks h-e-a-p high, water pony [boat] h-e-a-p buck!"

"Heap buck is right!" he gasped after a day of duckings, going overboard, fighting the crazy current, and dodging massive boulders.

Two days later the deafening noise began to wear on everyone but the Major. A few cursed it. The Major ignored it, outwardly at least. He could not sing or read poetry aloud these nights. No human voice could surmount the constant roaring. In this portion of the Green River, many creeks tumbled into it from lateral canyons, amid a wild confusion of rocks, trees, fallen timber, and thick underbrush. These gave access to the rim and were frequented by wild game. Hunting was good, and Sumner's marksmanship brought fresh meat to the monotonous diet of bacon, beans, and biscuit.

Day after day the boats bucked the river. When the Major commented, "I have the strangest feeling that the river seems to resent our being here," none of the men contradicted him.

He always scouted in advance for bad rapids. The men worried him because they no longer feared bad water; they relished the breakneck speed. The wilder the ride, the better! Knowing the months of travail ahead, the Major grew cautious, often irritating his crew because he made them line the boats frequently.

This was done by unloading each boat and attaching lines to the bow and stern. The bowline was carried from the shore to a point below the fall of water and secured around a boulder. The boat was then let down slowly by the men straining back on the sternline. When they could no longer hold against the pounding water, they let it go. The boat catapulted over the falls and was snubbed into shore by those waiting below. Countless trips were made, lugging supplies over the rocky, tilted shoreline to reload several tons of goods. It was tedious, exhausting work.

When the expedition reached Brown's Hole, the walls shunted back to form a small valley. At daybreak the Major woke to a chorus of warblers and meadowlarks. He lay in his blankets, luxuriating in bird-song. But not for long. "Time's a-wasting!" he roused his men.

For all the time Billy Hawkins spent on the water, he never changed his mess calls. "Roll out!" he yelled every morning in bullwhacker lingo. "Bulls in the corral! Chain up the gangs! Roll, you whackers!"

"Hang it, Billy, your cookin' is improvin'," Seneca Howland averred.

"It ain't neither," Bull Dunn insisted. "Those dang birds has made Seneca ringy!"

On June 7, hoisting himself over rocks hand and foot, the Major climbed a 2,000-foot cliff. He sat down, dangled his feet over the edge, and wrote letters to his family and Emma and the Chicago *Tribune.* "Heaven knows when I'll get these mailed, but just writing to the family makes me feel good."

Conscious of the audience he was addressing in the newspaper article, he did not spare the superlatives. "At noon the sun shone in splendor on its vermilion walls shaded into green and gray when the rocks are lichened over. The river fills the channel from wall to wall. The cañon opened like a beautiful portal to a region of glory. Now, as I write, the sun is going down, and the shadows are settling in the cañon. The vermilion gleams and the rosy hues, the green and gray tints, are changing to somber brown above, and black shadows below. Now 'tis a black portal to a region of gloom . . . the gateway through which we enter our voyage of exploration tomorrow . . ."

Though the one-armed former farm boy and schoolmaster, teetering on the edge of a chasm to write flowery prose, would not learn of it for months, already there were being circulated across the nation "eyewitness" accounts by spurious publicity-seekers who claimed that the Major and his party had already perished. Emma scorned the reports. Wes would have laughed too. "Why, we haven't tasted real danger yet," he would have said.

Disaster struck June 8 with stunning swiftness. About midday the Major was some distance in advance, scouting for bad water. He spotted a long rapid where the water boiled furiously in spinning funnels and treacherous cross-currents, and flagged wildly to those coming behind.

Sumner and Dunn cut hard for shore.

The Howland brothers and Goodman in the *No-Name* miscalculated. They were swept into the rapid and piled on a rock with such force they were thrown overboard. The boat teetered just long enough for them to grab the gunwale and haul themselves aboard.

The Major watched in agony as the boat was swept into another rapid, hit another rock, spun wildly, hit another rock broadside, and broke in two. The three men, struggling helplessly in the wild water, were swept out of sight.

Jumping onto the rocky shore, Major Powell led the race to the rescue, Sumner following with a rope. Around the bend they waded out and Sumner made an accurate toss, thanks to his years of throwing diamond hitches and roping horses. Dunn and Andy joined them in hauling the three half-drowned men to safety.

It was a costly mistake. The men were not only badly bruised by the pummeling on the rocks, but all their personal belongings were lost.

The blow affected every man. The Major announced, "One third of our entire food supply went down with the *No-Name*, and we're not yet one third through the canyon."

He tightened his belt. The others knew what he meant. No one objected to his calling this spot Disaster Falls.

CHAPTER THIRTEEN

RIMMED!

After Disaster Falls the men were less daring. They found rapid after rapid. Sun-blistered during the day, gasping in temperatures over 100 degrees, or buffeted by chill gales roaring through the canyon, they were never out of danger. The Major's clothes were never dry. His skin was rasped by the sand, parched by heat, his body bruised and sore, his hand raw from rope burns, his back muscles aching from over-exertion. The never-ceasing roar of the water exasperated him so that he found it difficult to remain even-tempered.

The valises and packing cases molded from constant wettings. The flour became wormy, the bacon rancid; the beans began to sprout.

The Major did not howl at each calamity. He felt he could not afford to do so: It was up to him to make little of the hardships. "Let a crew feel sorry for itself, and you're licked!" he realized. Nevertheless he tended their bruises and made them feel his personal concern for each man's welfare. To them the canyon passage was a job, and adventure. To Wes it was his life's goal, his great service to science and his country. Thus he had some relief from his misery, where the others did not. As Bradley complained unreasonably, "The Major is happy as long as he can geologize."

Yet he lost sleep worrying about his men and the souring

rations. They were not yet a month out of Green River, Wyoming, and their situation was becoming serious. "What will it be a month from now?" He shuddered and would not let himself think that possibly six to eight months were needed to run the canyons of the Colorado. Night after night he left his bedroll and paced the shoreline, giving himself wholly to prayer.

Only doubt never gnawed at him. Pain, discomfort, danger, worry — he knew these were the price for piercing the continent's last unexplored river. "Is it worth it?" he asked himself in lonely anguish one night. "Yes, a thousand times, yes!" his confidence asserted itself.

For several days his only note was, "Still rocks, rapids and portages." Five words describing untold hardship! Then the Green River relented. The canyon walls pushed back, the course was smoother. Through vast openings he looked out each side across a shimmering desert. Where grass grew along the river bank, the elk and deer grazing made good hunting.

The Major realized that his expedition had now run the canyons worn by the river through the great barrier of the Uintah Mountains, and he told the crew.

"We're making progress," Jack Sumner said, obviously pleased.

Andy Hall sighed contentedly. "Gee, this is a nice camp. The grass feels so good under my blanket. Let's celebrate with a song, Major."

"A song!" Goodman called out, raising his battered tin cup filled with Hawkins' turgid coffee. "Wet your vocal chords, Major, and have a go at it."

Leaning against a driftwood log, the campfire flicking golden lights on his dark red beard and sunburned nose, Wes sang snatches from the opera *Figaro*. Walter joined him on "Annie Laurie," and "Softly and Sweetly It Comes from Afar." The music soothed the men; the grim lines in their faces relaxed.

"We're makin' out all right," Billy spoke for all as he drifted off to sleep.

Disaster struck again the evening of June 17.

After the boats were pulled up on a bar lined with dry willow and scrub cedar, the Major and O. G. Howland, as usual, climbed the cliff to make their observations. Stopping to rest, they saw Billy Hawkins far below. "He's building that cookfire too close to the willows," the Major worried aloud.

A gust of wind scattered the flaming coals. The willows blazed, and fire raced the length of the bar. The men jumped for the boats, Hawkins stumbling with an armload of kettles and the mess kit. Before they could clear the lines, everyone was painfully singed. The current grabbed before the sweeps were set, and the boats shot a mile downstream before they could be brought to shore.

"Only a miracle kept those boats from being swamped," the Major said after he hurtled down the cliff and busied himself tending their burns.

Hawkins moaned the loss of the knives, forks, and spoons in the mess kit.

Andy laughed. "Shucks, we kin use our fingers. Think of the washin'-up you'll be saved."

The boats moved on to the place where the Yampa River flows into the Green. Here the Major sketched great hollow domes in the rock walls. High above he pointed to mountain sheep, as gray as the sandstone under their nimble feet.

Travel during the last days of June was good, in spite of the added trial of vicious mosquitoes. One day they made sixty-three miles "in a head-long ride." On June 28 the expedition reached the junction of the Uintah River with the Green.

"The first stage of the journey is now behind us," Powell told his men, smiling broadly. "Repair the boats and check all supplies and gear. I'm going thirty miles up the Uintah to the Indian agency. Give me any letters you want mailed, and Billy, make out a food list."

"I'll do better than that," Hawkins offered. "I'll go with you and help you tote the stuff back."

Frank Goodman spoke up. "I'll go with you too, but I won't be coming back." He had lost all his outfit in the wreck of the *No-Name.* "I've had enough of canyon travel, and the despicable food you serve up."

"As you wish," the Major told him, knowing that the men would not be sorry to lose the condescending Englishman.

At the Ute agency, the Major was dismayed to find the shelves almost bare of stock. He could buy only some flour. Returning, he and Hawkins found the others had already discarded the worst flour, the wormy beans, and two rancid hams. "The only thing we got a surplus of is rattlesnakes and scorpions," Seneca Howland grumbled.

Deeply concerned over their skimpy rations, the Major felt it only fair to give his men a chance to quit. "What do you want to do? Keep on with me, knowing you're going to have to get by on a meager handout of biscuits, beans, and dried apples? Or walk out to the agency and on to your homes?"

"I'm stayin'," one after another vowed, showing their faith in their leader.

Privately the Major confessed to Sumner, "We must complete the trip in four months, Jack, or give up for lack of food."

"You'll do it," the mountain man encouraged him.

Andy Hall dragged into camp about sunset, exhausted but proudly toting a haunch of venison on his shoulder. His friends went out to bring in the rest of the carcass. There were thick, juicy steaks and gravy for biscuits that night, and more for breakfast. The fresh meat helped to strengthen the men. The remainder was smoked to prevent spoilage.

Not far below Uintah the flotilla passed the mouth of the White River and touched an island where some Utes had planted a garden. "Mmmmm — stew!" Andy Hall murmured, rubbing his stomach. He called to the Major, "Fresh vegetables would be mighty tasty in venison stew."

"Help prevent scurvy," Bill Dunn added when he saw the Major hesitate.

The temptation was too great. The crew quickly raided the garden of small potatoes, carrots, beets, and turnips. Then they pushed off again and rowed vigorously until they were out of sight. An early stop was made for the midday meal.

"I don't know how to cook vegetables," Hawkins confessed. "I'm strictly a beans-and-biscuit man."

Andy advised confidently, "Oh, you throw the whole mess in the pot, tops 'n all, and let it boil. Add the venison and salt, and you got stew." It turned out to be bitter.

"But at least it's different," Seneca maintained good-naturedly.

About an hour later everyone was violently nauseated. The attack passed eventually, but the Major vowed weakly, "No more raiding gardens for me."

Two days of uneventful rowing followed. On July 8 the Major and Bradley left camp to measure the west wall of the canyon. It was steep and unusually dangerous to climb. Bradley carried the topographical level used for surveying so that the Major's one hand would be free. Although Wes was agile for a one-armed man, he suddenly found himself "rimmed" on a ledge, unable to advance or retreat. As he clung one-handed to the scrabbly rock wall, he looked back over his shoulder. The dizzying drop to the water almost made him ill and he called for help.

Bradley saw the trouble and climbed above the Major. There wasn't a tree limb to let down to the stranded man. All of the rope was in camp. Knowing that the sandstone would crumble under continued pressure, he inched his way to a terrace just above the Major, then shucked his drawers and lowered the baggy legs.

The Major looked at the lifesaving underwear dangling before his nose. He would have given a fortune for two good hands, one to dig into the wall, the other to grasp the cloth. Drops of perspiration ran down his forehead, blurring his sight, tickling his nose. He didn't dare sneeze! The slightest jarring movement would start the rocks sliding under him, and hurl him to his death.

"Steady, steady!" he told himself, gritting his teeth and taking several deep breaths. Pressing his body as close to the wall as possible, he released his grip. As he raised his arm, his body swayed backward. He grabbed the drawers in the nick of time. With a quick motion he turned his hand so the cloth wound over his wrist, giving him a better grip. "Pull!" he yelled to Bradley, who lay on his stomach. With super-human strength he raised the Major hand over hand until he lay sprawled on the safe ground.

"Thank God!" the Major gasped fervently as he lay there panting, almost sick with relief. But a few moments later he was on his feet, scrambling to the rim and using the topographical level. "Fifteen hundred and ninety-eight feet from rim to water! I would have had time to say my prayers before I hit bottom!"

Nine rapids were run successfully the next day, and then twenty more. Always on the lookout for fossils, because these were the keys to the geologic eras, the Major was thrilled to find some fossil teeth exposed in the canyon wall. "Aha! We're getting into deeper, older rock!" He knew that the teeth could only be found in a Paleozoic formation.

On July 11 the river tried to knock out the man who dared run its course. The *Emma Dean* was swamped in a rapid, the Major thrown overboard. He fought to keep his head above the rushing water and finally dog-paddled to shore. Sumner and Dunn reclaimed the boat, but the rifles, bedding, and one barometer were lost. Even before his clothes stopped dripping, the Major was whittling away on new oars from driftwood. "On we go!" he shouted, his zest unquenchable.

Through July 14, 15, and 16 the river dwaddled like a fussy woman, the flaming orange cliffs carved deep by ancient erosion into domed amphitheaters. Climbing to the rim, Wes looked out over the desert sand. "Look at those colors," he gasped, ignoring the sun that sucked the moisture from his skin. The sand was orange, reddish brown, white, with no sprig of living green brush to relieve the harshness. Flat-bedded mesas and buttes rode like mighty ships across this desert, their sides banded in formations of blue, yellow, pink, purple. "If people saw an artist's painting of this country, they'd think he was painting a dream world." He regretted that the most he could do was make crude geological sketches, fine-lined, sparse, with tiny pencil strokes to hint at the variations in color.

On the afternoon of July 16 the Major's pilot boat began bobbing on the crests of swelling waves. "We must be nearing the junction," he mentioned to Jack Sumner.

The mountain man, gaunt, his teeth gleaming through sun-blistered lips, bore down on his oars so that they shot along. "Can't get there soon enough to suit me," he said.

The junction was that of the Grand, whose upper reaches Sumner and the Major had explored the previous winter, and the Green that would soon be past history to them. The Utes had told them that the Grand poured into the Green over a mighty waterfall. Instead, they discovered that it flowed "in a calm, strong tide." The Major's flag flickered gaily, and the boats pulled to shore.

"We've made it two-thirds of the way, boys!" he shouted to his crew. "Now take it easy for a few days while I sketch. Then we'll tackle the big one, the Grand Canyon."

CHAPTER FOURTEEN

THE GRAND CANYON
OF THE COLORADO

"Rocks everywhere, and no vegetation," the Major described the area at the junction of the Grand and Green. "No soil; no sand . . . a whole land of naked rock, with giant forms carved on it . . ." While he geologized from dawn to dusk, the crew recaulked the boats and sifted the moldy flour through mosquito netting. Two hundred pounds had to be discarded. "Good-by, biscuits that never were," Andy clowned as the flour skimmed away.

Billy Hawkins picked up the theodolite and squinted through it. Knowing that the cook had no idea how to use the complex surveying instrument, Powell asked, "What are you doing, Billy?"

"Sightin' the latitude and longitude to the nearest pie!"

On July 21 the Major gave the signal, "Cast off!" and the boats took out into the cocoa-colored, silt-heavy Colorado River. It was the same old story of fast water, dangerous rapids, sweating portages. "The water is worsening, if that's possible," he said to Jack Sumner. The rapids were monstrous, the portaging exhausting for a leader and crew whose prime strength was already weakened by too much exertion or too little food.

Repeatedly the boats were swamped, oars splintered, a rapid run blind with the Major's heart in his mouth. "I've lost all respect for those canyons upstream," he gasped as the pilot boat survived a terror that he named Cataract Canyon. The thunder of rocks bowling along the river bed reminded him of the heavy cannonading during the siege of Vicksburg. "But it's not all bad," he encouraged his crew, "we may be wet, weary, and hungry —— "

"But we're willing!" Andy interrupted. "Heck, none of us figgered this trip for a picnic."

Sumner shot two bighorn sheep. Billy fried the steaks and made gravy for the biscuits. The Major ate until he could only stretch on the beach and groan from the almost forgotten pleasure of having a full stomach.

Once more the river relented in a long stretch of easy water. The walls lowered some. The salmon-colored sandstone cliffs were streaked with brown desert varnish.

"I'm calling this Glen Canyon because it is so beautiful and serene," the Major said. On the hardest days even he lacked the reserve energy to climb the walls and sketch the back country. There were increasing gaps in his daily journals and scientific observations. However much he regretted these omissions, he made no outward sign. "The men are doing their best. I can't ask for more."

Farther along he wrote, "Clouds are playing in the cañon today. Sometimes they roll down in great masses, filling the gorge with gloom; sometimes they hang above from wall to wall, and cover the cañon with a roof of impending storm . . . Then, a gust of wind sweeps down a side gulch, and making a rift in the clouds, reveals the blue heavens, and a stream of sunlight pours in."

Early morning and late afternoon colors were staggering, ever-changing pale yellow deepening to orange, pink to red, lavender to purple. At dawn the canyon literally exploded in color, as if a giant paint pot had suddenly spilled down the walls, coating pyramids, rock temples, fluted towers, and rainbow bridges. During midday the colors flattened out, muted in the brassy sunshine. Then as the sun retreated behind far-distant mountains, the colors deepened till blue shadows rose from the bottom and lowered from the rim, extinguishing everything in a languid blackness.

In this area the Major discovered his first Moqui (Hopi) ruins. As usual, he was standing on the deck of the pilot boat, peering up at the vast amphitheaters worn in the canyon walls. Suddenly he noticed what appeared to be a huge cavern, with buildings in it. He blinked. "Good heavens, I must be crazy with the heat!" He looked again, hard and long, then signaled excitedly for the boats to pull to shore.

"Whats' up?" Sumner asked.

"A village of some sort, high up on the rocks!"

The mountain man eyed his leader. "The old boy's cracking up," he thought. But he followed the Major as he climbed the rock wall by means of age-old steps chipped in the sandstone. The Major reached the floor of the cavern and stepped aside for his men. He was speechless, awe-struck. Here before him was a many-storied, flat-faced dwelling of sun-baked adobe, with walls and terraces of the same material and ladders stretching from one level to another. Fatigue melted away. He surged forward to examine every room, sketching dimensions frantically. Under his direction the crew gathered pieces of ancient pottery and baskets, and a few skulls, handling them with unusual delicacy. Powell's heart beat wildly. He had made an unexpected, fascinating discovery, a rich reward for any explorer.

But time and hunger forced him to leave. "I'm coming back," he vowed. "I don't know how or when, but I'll never rest until I've made an exhaustive survey of this cliff dwelling."

The boats passed the mouth of the Paria River, an ancient fording used by the Indians, now known as Lee's Ferry. The Major squinted down a heartbreakingly long stretch of white water. A lesser man would have left the river here, where an Indian trail led out to civilization.

"Do we go on?" he asked his men. The prospect was so dim,

his men so weary, that he felt that their welfare and wishes must be considered before his own burning wish to continue on through the canyon.

"You willin', Major?" Bill Dunn asked, wiping his sweat off his face with a callused, bony hand.

"I am," he answered without the slightest hesitation.

"Then let's go!" Andy Hall croaked through swollen, blistered lips.

After they had come through with the usual wettings and bruises, the Major called this Marble Canyon, "one of the deadliest on the entire river." It cut through a wilderness flanked on the west by the Vermilion and Echo Cliffs, and behind them the long, high, wind-swept limestone Kaibab Plateau.

At the mouth of the Little Colorado, "a loathesome little stream at this time of the year," they camped for two days. Near there, at water level, Powell noted red limestone shot through with dikes of lava. "Proterozoic formation," he said enthusiastically to Bradley. "We're getting deeper. We're not far from the black Archeozoic granite."

The two climbed and rooted around in a greenish-gray shale until the Major found a trilobite. "Paleozoic!" he identified its era. He struggled toward the top, past beds of limestone and sandstone, some hundreds of feet thick, gray, buff, red, then crossed the plateau and climbed to the top of a mesa. "Here's brown conglomerate formed during the Mesozoic era." He could scarcely contain his joy. "Imagine seeing formations of all but the oldest geologic eras exposed to the naked eye. Do you realize that we have just climbed up millions upon millions upon millions of years of history?"

Bradley nodded indifferently. Hardship and hunger had dulled his zest for exploration. He whined constantly, not outwardly but in his diary. He criticized the Major for ignoring his men's welfare, a wholly false complaint and one the others did not share.

That night Powell announced, "The walls rise three thousand feet above the river now. Judging by my calculations, we start running the Grand Canyon tomorrow."

"How long do you figure it is, Major?" Andy wanted to know.

"At least two hundred miles. Maybe more."

The thought of the dreadful distance pressed on the men's spirits. "Two hundred through the canyon or to the nearest outpost?"

"Two hundred to the Virgin River and the end of the journey," the Major explained. "I understand there are Mormons settled along the Virgin. We ought to find someone to feed us there."

Food! Only two hundred miles away! Eyes brightened, backs straightened.

"We're on the home stretch!" Billy Hawkins hollered.

Everyone cheered but the Howland brothers. "Two hundred more miles of this?" O.G. gasped to Seneca, his words smothered by the cheers. "I can't take much more!"

"We got no choice," Seneca said grimly.

The water wheeled and boiled, the walls soared higher, the channel narrowed. O.G. grew more and more tense until one day he screamed, "This is worse than any rocky prison! We'll never come out of it alive!"

The Major tried to soothe him, as did the others, but it was no use. O.G. walked off by himself and brooded.

When the deepest rocks of all time, the black Archeozoic granite — huge, tilted slabs of it — engorged the river, the Major took scant time to study them. Here was one of the great thrills he had anticipated, sketching these rocks. "But the men are starving, and getting so weak they can hardly row. I can't stop here. I've got to shoot the Grand Canyon as quickly as possible!" So he limited himself to meager notes and prayed that his once-phenomenal memory would serve him later on.

There were chilly, rainy days, and others when all gasped in

125-degree temperatures. Rocks, rapids, whirlpools, the maddening roar of the water, walls *over a mile high now*, all depressed men surviving on biscuits and coffee.

O.G. finally cracked. "I refuse to go farther on this river! It's suicide or murder!" he lashed out, his bloodshot eyes wild. "Look at that rapid ahead there. We can't get through it without the boats breaking in two. I'm not going to drown like a rat. I'm getting out overland!"

"An' I'm goin' with him," Seneca supported his brother.

Bill Dunn shuffled his feet. "Me too. I gotta get away from this canyon or go crazy."

The Major pleaded with them, but he might as well have talked to the rocks. "We can't be far from the Grand Wash Cliffs and the Virgin." He was speaking from knowledge gained previously in studying the journal of an exploration of the Lower Colorado from the Gulf of California to the Virgin.

"We'll take our chances crossing the desert," the Howlands and Dunn insisted stubbornly.

Their last night together, the Major could not sleep. He walked up and down the beach, praying that the unknown terrors of the next few days could be surmounted, that the three men would survive the desert. "It's no longer a race to get out of the canyon," he faced the truth starkly. "It's a race with death."

The next morning he told his crew, "Any of you who want to go with the Howlands are free to do so." None hesitated to remain with him. "All right," he gasped, their loyalty bringing him almost to tears. "Billy, make up the last of the flour into biscuits and split them among the Howlands and us."

After being supplied with guns and ammunition, O.G. and Seneca and Dunn shook hands all around and climbed the cliff. From the rim high above, they waved and disappeared from sight. The Major marked the place as Separation Rapids.

Now that they were short-handed, he abandoned the *Emma Dean*. Somehow he led the *Sister* and the *Maid* through the boiling rapids. "We never had such a rapid before, but we have run a worse one this afternoon," he wrote in his trembling hand.

It was some time before the Major noticed a change in the canyon. Ever so gradually it widened, the walls retreated, more than a narrow ribbon of sky could be seen. Finally through a V-slotted opening, he glimpsed brown desert. "We're running out of the granite!" he shouted through swollen, bleeding lips.

The river quieted.

Billy Hawkins perked up when he heard a bird call.

The towering Grand Wash Cliffs swung past.

The river's threat was over. Late in the afternoon of August 30 the Major spotted the red mudflats of the Virgin River. "Look ahead," he shouted.

The men squinted through bloodshot eyes, then croaked, "It's over! We made it! We made it!" They pounded each other's backs with bony fists.

A white man and two boys, fishing with nets, waded out in answer to the Major's summons, and hauled the battered boats onto dry land. They were Mormons who had been ordered by their leader, Brigham Young, to be on the lookout for survivors or wreckage of the Powell expedition. Their strong hands guided the exhausted leader and his companions to a cabin nearby where they were seated at a table and ate their first real meal in weeks.

"Cream!" the Major cried out, almost too weak to lift a small pitcher and enrich his coffee.

"Butter, by gad!" Sumner gasped, slathering it on "risin" bread. He wolfed down venison steak, potatoes, squash. Andy Hall blubbered when given a slice of melon. He buried his mouth in the cool, sweet, moist pulp.

After he had eaten, the Major staggered outside. "How big the sky is! How sweet the bird's evensong!" He rubbed green leaves of a plant on his face. How wonderful the rich smell of growing things.

Soon the men joined him, and all returned to the boats. For a

while they lay contentedly around the campfire, talking over
the long voyage.

Over and over the Major murmured worriedly, "I wonder
how O.G. and Seneca and Bill are making out."

"Dawgonnit, I wish they'd stuck with us," Billy Hawkins said.

Finally they were gabbed out and stretched under the worn
blankets. The Major had his first real sleep in weeks.

The magnificent exploration was over. The blank spaces in
the maps could be filled in now that a one-armed commander
and a lusty-spirited, rack-boned crew had conquered the might-
iest river of the West!

CHAPTER FIFTEEN

ROCKING CHAIR OR SADDLE?

On September 1, 1869, the Powell expedition was officially disbanded. The Major divided what little money he had among his crew. Men who had shared untold experiences separated, never to meet again. Jack Sumner, Bradley, Andy Hall, and Billy Hawkins gathered more supplies and ran the river down to the Gulf of California. The Major and Walter headed out to Salt Lake City.

The Mormons provided them with horses and sent runners out to check on the Howlands and Dunn. Meanwhile the *Desert Telegraph* relayed the good news to the outer world that Major John Wesley Powell and five of his comrades had successfully completed their exploration.

Anxious as he was to rejoin Emma and his family, the Major waited at Salt Lake City for news of the men who had taken the long risk at Separation Rapids. When the word came, it was bad. O. G. Howland, his brother Seneca, and Bill Dunn had gambled and lost. Due to a tragic misunderstanding, they were murdered by Shivwit Indians. Even now their bodies, bristling with arrows, lay somewhere out on the naked wasteland.

Realizing that it would be months before the details were known, the Major decided to journey eastward. "But I'll be back," he told his Mormon friends. Because he could not bear the thought of three good friends' bodies lying exposed to the

harsh desert sunlight, he asked if a party could go out and give
them decent burial and retrieve any papers or diaries found on
them.

"We'll do it," they promised.

The Major next found himself catapulted into fame. "You're
a national hero!" Walter kept saying when his brother received
a celebrity's welcome everywhere.

Thanks to the spurious "eyewitness" reports published earlier
about the entire expedition perishing in the Flaming Gorge of
the Green, considerable attention had been focused on the
daring one-armed adventurer. The public admired his boldness,
adored his gaunt, slight stature, thought his being maimed, his
auburn hair, and his beard were "romantic." The Major had
never lost his boyish habit of blushing, though the red flush
showed little on his weathered face.

"Brave!"

"Dauntless!"

"Magnetic!"

Superlatives poured over him.

"Emma!" was the word he longed to shout, and soon jumped
off the train before it came to a full stop at Detroit and swept
his wife in his arms.

She was ecstatically happy. Her handsome Wes was a hero,
a great explorer! She had kept herself busy and cheerful during the long separation. "At last we'll be settling down," she
exclaimed, "after your lecture tour, of course." She would not
deprive him of his hour of glory. And she was practical. A
celebrity could command a high price for platform appearances,
and the money would be a welcome addition to the lean family
budget.

They traveled to Chicago, where the Major's lectures were
repeated over and over to enthusiastic crowds. He spoke in a
modest and straightforward manner, and gave fair credit to his
crew. Then he and Emma moved on to Wheaton for a big
family reunion.

"Now that Wes has had his fill of travel," Emma chatted happily to her in-laws, "we can settle down and live like other couples. Wes is bound to be offered a fine professorship somewhere."

But John Wesley Powell had other plans, although his adoring wife didn't know it yet. The placid waters of academic life and a professorship had no challenge for the man who had collected shells along the Mississippi River, topped Long's Peak, and conquered the Colorado.

Even before leaving the Mormon cabin on the Virgin River, he had decided to return to the great river. The sudden onslaught of fame had not dimmed his innate honesty. When it came to evaluating his work, he was ruthless. "I've known from the start this was not a bona-fide scientific expedition," he told himself. "I left too many gaps that must be filled in."

During the hours he had spent scouring the country back from the canyon rim, asking himself the scientific explanation for the buttes and mesas, the high-altitude plateau and its maze of canyons, he had begun to evolve a new and revolutionary theory. The current supposition was the usual one — the plateau had been thrust up eons ago, and the canyons, particularly the Colorado, were eroded after that by a river chewing deeper and deeper into the sandstone, limestone, shale, and granite formations.

After observing minutely the beds exposed from the top of the isolated mesas down to the black Archeozoic granite, he had found proof that *the river had been there in the beginning,* before the massive upheaval, and had been lifted along with the plateau and mountains and had continued its erosive action from its new elevation. He sensed but did not know positively yet, for lack of information and study, that the canyons and vast dry-land plateau comprising the western slopes of Colorado, the eastern and southern expanse of Utah, and northern portions of Arizona and New Mexico were bound together not only in geological history, but in a distinctive, highly individualistic economic entity. But there had not been time enough to work out his theory. Science had not been served, as he had dreamed. Spoiled food, battered boats, rapids, and cataracts — survival, not science, dominated the closing weeks on the river.

As he mulled his ideas over in his mind, he realized, "The trip down the Colorado was only opening a door to something bigger."

Other men had crossed this canyon country overland without seeing the values inherent in the dry-land empire. The Major did not belittle these men their superb courage and resourcefulness and their grim survivals. But now he knew how limited were their visions: the Spanish *conquistadores* seeking the fabulous, legendary cities of gold; the Spanish priests carrying the banner of the Roman Catholic faith to primitive peoples; the traders blazing a route of commerce; the military seeking fortifications; the gold-seekers and land-hungry pioneers driving the Indians from the river bottoms; yes, even the scientists of three federal survey parties already mapping the fringe of this "wasteland." It was a desperate land, promising little mineral wealth and opportunity for settlement. Thus men of limited vision saw only a fraction of its worth.

Now John Wesley Powell's footsteps were on this land, a man who was devout but not a priest; conqueror of a river but not of men; uninterested in trade routes, gold deposits, grass; untrained, as compared to the experts traveling with the three federal scientific surveys. Had he been asked, he would have said, "I am interested in filling the blank spaces of my country's maps, in learning all I can about the forests, insects, rocks, birds, and Indians of this region." He should have added, "I don't care two hoots about being a celebrity."

Many months later, after further hardship, travel, and intensive study, he would realize that not only had he explored a river — he had discovered a new province, *the plateau province.*

Now he saw only the immediate future. Lectures and social gatherings soon became unbearable. He felt that the time had come to tell Emma his plans. "I've got to run the river again. There was so much I didn't do."

Emma nearly fainted. "But you barely survived!"

After she had rallied, Wes went on determinedly: "I plan to organize a second expedition to the Colorado. I shall seek a congressional appropriation to underwrite the cost. I shall ask the museum directors to continue my salary for one more year."

Emma choked back her tears. "You've got it all planned, haven't you?"

Wes nodded. Then his eyes sparkled, and his cheeks flushed as he said, "We've got to work out details for better equipment and locate supply stations along the river." He smiled boyishly at her. "We've got a thousand things to do!"

"We've got a thousand things to do!"

Emma smiled. Her rosy dreams disappeared in a bright flood of excitement as she was swept once more into the mainstream of her husband's career. "Maybe I'll never have a nice home on a tree-lined street in some quiet college town," she thought. "But is that what I really want? Do I want a rocking chair and faculty tea parties, or a saddle on an Indian pony and mountain trout fried over pine coals?"

"I want Wes!" her heart shouted within her. "His restless service to science, his absorption in natural history, his whirl-wind enthusiasm . . . his deep devotion to me."

Impulsively she kissed him. "When do we leave for Washington? What letters can I write for you?" She was already ticking off in her mind all that she could do to help her husband.

CHAPTER SIXTEEN

PAIUTES AND PUEBLOS

In June, 1870, Major Powell obtained a 10,000-dollar appropriation for a survey of the Colorado and its tributaries. Three other government surveys were working in the West then: the War Department's Survey of the Fortieth Parallel directed by Clarence King, and Survey West of the 110th Meridian under Lieutenant George W. Wheeler; the Interior Department's Survey of the Territories headed by Dr. Ferdinand Vandiveer Hayden. The Powell Survey, as it was known hereafter, came under the Interior Department.

The King, Wheeler, and Hayden surveys had highly trained scientists on their staffs. Although outstanding specialists volunteered for his survey, the Major by-passed them again in favor of relatives, students, and amateurs.

"I'd like you to be my right-hand man," he asked his brother-in-law, Harry Thompson, now a school principal at Bloomington, Illinois. "You're a bear for detail, and that's what I want in a chief topographer. If I furnish you with my field notes, will you draft the base map for our operations?"

Thompson was delighted. The westering bug had bitten him on the 1868 trip. Deep within his unassuming, bookish exterior was a desire to emulate his famous brother-in-law's exploits. "Leave it to me," he said.

The Major delivered the field notes. Then he and Emma left

for Salt Lake City. "I've two immediate problems," he told her on the lengthy train ride. "One is to establish good relations with the Indians so that none of our men need run afoul of an attack such as the Howlands and Dunn suffered. The other is to locate supply points along the river. I know the Green is easily accessible by pack train into Brown's Hole, the Uintah River route, the old Spanish Crossing, and the Paria. But I'm going to need others near and below Cataract Canyon. One, in particular, down the Dirty Devil, will probably take some hunting.

Emma smiled to herself. The innocent little phrase, "will take some hunting," didn't fool her. She knew it meant that Wes would prowl the wilderness and canyons, "and love every minute of it." Long ago she had learned not to fret about her husband's ventures into the primitive wilds. "He's practically indestructible," she consoled herself. "Wes would die a thousand deaths if he were chained to a desk."

Aloud she said, "You dictate the letters you want written, and the supply lists, and I'll draft the work outline."

Impulsively Wes squeezed her hand. "When I think of the hundreds of letters you have written for me, the hours of work you have saved me!"

"I love it!" she said gaily. "It keeps me in close touch with you. I feel I have a big share in your career that way. I like being my husband's right hand."

Wes blushed in spite of his thirty-six years. Then he said softly, "I don't think I ever told you, but I had some pretty dark hours in the canyon. It took a lot of praying to get through there, Emma. When I was most discouraged, I would come across some notes you had copied for me, and suddenly I wasn't alone any more. You were there with me!"

Emma's heart pounded. Wes wasn't the most romantic husband in the world, and she treasured these rare moments.

"I'm going to be working more and more in the canyon country," he continued. "We'll be separated for months at a time.

I — I thought you'd like to know that, wherever you are, you're with me too, out in the field."

Once they were settled in a small apartment in Salt Lake City, the Major called on Brigham Young. The great Mormon leader was intensely interested in Powell's explorations because the Saints had taken up settlement in the vast desert, much of it uncharted.

After a friendly visit Young advised, "If you want to make peace with the Indians along the river, go south to Kanab, Utah. Contact Jacob Hamblin, my missionary leader there. He knows those Indians as no other man does. If he trusts you, he will serve as your guide and interpreter."

The Major rushed home and packed his field kit, a worn valise containing rough clothing, notebooks, and pencils. Emma asked, "How long will you be gone?" He laughed, "Until I get back." At a nearby stable he rented a saddle horse and rode south to Kanab, an outpost where industrious Mormons were converting the desert into rich farms by means of irrigation ditches.

Jacob Hamblin towered above the Major, his six feet two inches of brawn straining his buckskin suit. He had dedicated himself to establishing peace between the Shoshones, Utes, Hopis, and the whites in the territory being taken over by the Mormons.

The Major presented Young's letter of introduction. "You have heard, no doubt, about the Shivwits' murdering three men from my first expedition," he said. "I'm very concerned about the security of those of my second expedition which will get under way next May. Is there some way this trouble with the Shivwits can be settled?"

"You want to punish the Shivwits?"

"No," was the emphatic answer. "I want to find out why they murdered my men, and arrange a peace to prevent further trouble. I don't want retribution of any sort."

"Then I'll take you to them," the buckskin apostle agreed.

The next morning the two rode out across the jumbled desert country, Hamblin whang-leather tough from years of wilderness travel, Powell bristling with energy. The route followed the valley of the Sevier River to its headwaters, and from there to the foot of the soaring Pink Cliffs on the Upper Kanab River.

"We'll establish our base camp here," Hamblin advised, unpacking their tent and meager equipment.

The Major purposely moved slowly into this new country. He was like a man possessed as he mapped the Badlands. It was his nature to learn from everything he saw, touched, and studied, mile upon mile, every hour, every day.

It didn't take Hamblin long to gain a profound respect for his slight companion who proved to be rugged, uncomplaining, and an enthusiastic talker around the campfire. At sunset they lingered over their coffee. The pink, yellow, and white sedimentary bandings of the Pink Cliffs reminded Powell of a strawberry parfait. "An ice cream sundae desert-style!" he joked. Then he noticed a thin finger of smoke spiral above the horizon. He sat up, alert. "What have we got there? A forest fire?"

"Kaibabits signaling," the missionary told him, unperturbed. "Look for company tomorrow."

He was right. The next day the Kaibabits straggled slowly out from one of the tangled gulches nearby.

The Major watched them approaching over the blistered rock, noting their small stature, low foreheads, lank hair, and filthy rags. Suddenly he wished he could provide a feast of venison and beans and let them eat until they could hold no more. "Even the youngest ones look old. Not one of them looks as if he ever had enough to eat."

He stood by Hamblin as the missionary greeted Chief Chuarruumpeak. The tall apostle and the wizened Kaibabit leader exchanged compliments before the Major was introduced and his mission explained. With great dignity the Indian invited the white men to join his tribesmen for further talk. Before he was even settled on the harsh, hot ground, the Major had his notebook and stub pencil in his hand.

Hamblin translated after a while: "Because I ask it, they will show you the water holes. They say you cannot get to the river from here." He added, chuckling, "The medicine man wants a few snips of your red hair. Would you mind?"

Powell obliged, scarcely concealing his amusement. What would his father say if he knew his Methodist-reared son's hair would find its way into an Indian medicine pouch? "Tell Chuarruumpeak I like him and his people very much and want to write down their old-man stories. Have you asked if he will help us contact the Shivwits?"

"Later, my friend."

The Major was content. He didn't want to rush things. "I'll put the time to good use."

Days later he had pages of notes. He traded some trinkets for pottery and handcraft which he knew Professor Henry of the Smithsonian would be grateful to receive. Having mastered a few words of the language, he overheard Hamblin ask the chief to take them to the Shivwits. The chief agreed readily and led them across the sun-baked, present-day boundary between Utah and Arizona. Moving slowly under the burning sun, they toiled up onto a mesa called Uinkaret, Place of Pines. From this vast lava-capped, pine-crowned butte, Powell looked across the broken country to the chasm of the Colorado. Somewhere out there, in a hidden "hole," were the Shivwits. The trail landmarks were known only to the Indians. The surface of the land looked as if it had been gashed and chewed by some monstrous prehistoric tiger.

Soon a runner, summoned by smoke signals, appeared. After talking with Chuarruumpeak, he indicated that he would guide the white men to his people, the Uinkarets, as primitive a tribe as Powell would ever visit. Chuarruumpeak and his people bade them farewell and withdrew.

Once more the Major had to allow time for the Uinkarets to get to know him. Fortunately theirs was a Ute dialect, and he and Hamblin knew enough words so that they could communicate fairly easily. The Indians became fascinated with this man who "made many scratches with stick." They had no scribe, and none of them had ever seen a man write.

The squaws giggled when he asked them what seeds they roasted. He watched them pound insects to fatten their meal cakes. "Good, good!" he complimented gamely after he had sampled them.

Solemn, black-eyed babies, propped in baskets wrapped with wildcat skins, gurgled when he cooed at them. The young men staged a rabbit drive and races in his honor. The chief gave him a Uinkaret name. "You, Ka-pur-ats," he said, driving a bony finger into Powell's chest.

"What does that mean?" the Major asked the missionary.

"One-Arm-Off," was the answer.

A few days later he admitted, "Geology is certainly getting a passing swipe on this trip. I'm so absorbed recording these Indian songs and dances and old-man stories that I don't even think about rocks."

Hamblin chuckled. "You'll have more fresh material tomorrow. The chief tells me the Shivwits should arrive by then." Powell hadn't known they had been summoned.

The Shivwits approached cautiously. They were uneasy and suspicious of the white men. However, once they were seated in a circle, Jacob Hamblin rose and in his kind voice told them about the Major. "Kapurats is not looking for gold," he assured them, using sign language when words failed him. "He does not want your land. He wants to be friends and learn all about you."

The Uinkaret chief rose and said the same thing. When the Shivwits indicated that they understood, he sat down.

Hamblin resumed. "Next year Kapurats will travel the red river in his water pony. He does not want Shivwits to kill his men. They are good men. They do not want gold. They do not want land." Over and over he stressed, "Kapurats does not want revenge. He only wants to know why you killed his brothers."

Timidly, in hang-dog fashion, the Shivwit chief spoke for his people: They were sorry; they had mistaken Kapurats' brothers for prospectors who had murdered one of the squaws. They did not torture the men, but killed them while they slept. They would not molest any more of Kapurats' brothers. Would he smoke the pipe?

The Major nodded, but gulped as it was passed to him. The pipe had a large stem, broken long ago and mended with a buckskin rag tied on with sinew. The cracked mouthpiece was also wound with rags, and wet from the chief's sucking on it.

"I can't put that to my mouth!" Powell groaned to himself. "It looks like the burying ground for centuries of dead spittle! Ground insects in meal cakes I can face, but not this!"

To gain time he filled the pipe with some of his own tobacco, then engaged in very earnest conversation with the chief, with much hand-waving and quick passes at his lips, and then gave it back. With profuse apology he indicated that he had talked so long the pipe was no longer smoking. Quickly striking a match, he made great ceremony of lighting it. The chief's chest swelled. What an honor the white man was paying him, he told his tribesmen. The Major sighed with relief when the chief passed the pipe on to his medicine man.

In talking further with the Shivwits, he asked, "Are there any pueblos near here? I would like to visit one." He had never forgotten the pueblo ruins discovered in the canyon.

Hamblin perked up his ears. "I've never seen one. Offer the chief a few coins and see if he will provide us with a guide."

The Major did so, and soon he and Hamblin were riding away from the Uinkarets and Shivwits. After a five-day journey across the desert they came to the old town of Oraibi, a Hopi village in almost primitive condition. It was a rare compliment, Powell realized, for him to be taken to a place revered by the red men. Later he was taken to others almost inaccessible on the flat-topped mesas. He took full advantage of the opportunity. He forgot about the plans for the Colorado expedition. Hoping Emma wouldn't mind his staying away for so long, he gave complete, selfless absorption to his study of the pueblos.

For two months he worked from dawn to darkness, and by firelight, until Hamblin called a halt.

"Oh, dear," Powell remembered. "I haven't looked for that supply route down the Dirty Devil to the foot of Cataract Canyon. Do you think you might locate it, Hamblin?"

"I'll try," the missionary promised.

On the return trip to Kanab, the Major labored on his geological sketches, if only to assuage guilty feelings for having neglected his ultimate plan to map the entire canyon and plateau province.

When he forwarded the rough field sketches to Harry Thompson back in Illinois, he wrote, "I have decided on Kanab as winter headquarters for the survey."

Then he said good-by to Hamblin. "Now back to Salt Lake City and Mrs. Powell. But I will return."

CHAPTER SEVENTEEN

THE SECOND COLORADO EXPEDITION

On May 22, 1871, Major John Wesley Powell waited for his crew to assemble on the river bank at Green River Crossing, Wyoming. He had just put Emma on the train to Salt Lake City where she would await his return. "It's a low-water year, and our boats are better designed and equipped. Don't worry about me."

"I won't," she promised. "But don't you worry about me either." Emma was expecting their first child and had found the last month of whirlwind preparations a little exhausting. "I'll have Nellie to look after me." Nellie was her husband's sister who was married to Harry Thompson, the chief topographer for the second Colorado expedition.

After the train pulled out, the Major returned to the river bank. Profiting by the shortcomings of the first expedition, he had designed sturdier rowboats with waterproof lockers and partial decks of wood or canvas. An American flag with the boat's name embroidered on the field of blue rippled from the jackstaffs of the *Emma Dean II*, the *Nellie Powell*, and the *Cañonita*. "Maybe we are a 'Cinderella Survey,'" he admitted honestly, using the nickname given his survey by newspaper reporters because of its skimpy appropriation and roster of amateurs. But he vowed, "We're going to do more for science than the King, Wheeler, and Hayden surveys put together!"

According to his last check everything was in readiness: supplies and equipment stowed in rubber sacks, the 1,100 pounds of flour, beans, dried apples and tinned peaches, tea, coffee, sugar, salt and bacon divided among the three craft. Each man had been allowed one hundred pounds' weight of extra clothing and shoes, blankets, a rifle, and ammunition. The crew would be along as soon as they filled up on ham and eggs at Jake's Eatery.

He was comfortably attired in cotton overalls and shirt, sturdy shoes and a dilapidated hat. In order to have scouting aboard the *Emma II* less strenuous, he had bolted a *rocking chair,* with a life preserver looped over one arm, to a small platform in the middle of the pilot boat. The crew had joked about his being an "armchair explorer," but he hadn't thought it amusing. He was deadly serious in all that concerned his scientific work; otherwise he was good-natured most of the time. However, he abhorred laziness, whining, and carelessness and was sharp in expressing his disapproval of such.

As he squinted up at the turquoise sky, he wished the crew would hurry. For canyon experience, all but Walter were tenderfeet and anxious to experience the roaring rapids of the inner canyons. They had complete confidence in their leader because he had run the river once and had arranged supply points so there would be no threat of starvation. The Major grunted. "They're leaving all the worrying to me! No matter, I'm used to it."

It was ten o'clock before he called, "Shove off!" The first ten miles were leisurely, particularly for a leader piloting from a rocking chair. That first night he chose a campsite among some greasewoods. Before long Andy Hattan, no bullwhacker as Billy Hawkins had been, hollered, "Come 'n git it!" The Major led the parade around the cookfire. Supper consisted of bacon, strong tea, and excellent biscuits.

Before bedtime that night, and the many that followed, he read poetry aloud by firelight, especially passages from *The*

Lady of the Lake, and led the singing. Sleep came easily after he rolled in his blankets, lulled by the wind soughing over the cliffs and the throaty suck of the Green.

The next morning he was full of pepper. While others made the usual scientific observations of longitude and latitude, temperature, mileage, barometric pressure, and stream flow, and Harry Thompson began his careful mapping of the Green, the Major explored the rimrock country. Seventeen-year-old Fred Dellenbaugh, a competent artist, accompanied him so that he was freed of much of the burden of sketching.

This trip he had brought along a photographer. E. O. Beaman and his assistant were hard put to keep up with him. The camera was large and cumbersome. Strip film or dry-plate processing had not yet been introduced, so Beaman used the wet-plate process. As soon as a plate was exposed, he rushed it to the portable dark box and developed it. Fortunately the scenery was so extraordinary that even his uninspired photographs sold well later as stereopticon slides.

The crew suffered few discomforts, save one fellow, Richardson. "Something is always happening to Frank," the Major said the first few times Richardson fell overboard or tripped on rocks or skinned his hands and knees. Then one evening he sat on a hot coal and ignited his trousers. Jerking to his feet, he yelled, "Fire!" and jumped into the river. Everyone laughed except the Major, who was annoyed. He realized that Richardson was bumbling and helpless and might blunder into a serious accident. "I shouldn't have let his being a friend of the family influence me in permitting him to join us," he confided to Walter. "He's really a nuisance." Then he shrugged. Beyond cautioning Richardson, he could do little.

Soon the boats reached the crossing at Brown's Hole. As he stepped ashore, the Major was astonished to find two ranchers there, eager for news and willing to swap fresh beef for flour. "You've settled this far out?" he asked as they drank coffee together.

"Got to!" one rancher said. "With pretty dang near half the nation movin' westward since the war, a man's got to scratch to find good river bottom and grassland. This is a good hole for fattenin' cattle."

"We're lucky," his companion added. "Least we got grass and water. That's more 'n the poor devils have who are tryin' to settle on the fringe areas, and gamble on what little rain there is to save their crops."

The Major was disturbed. He knew that the West was being flooded with settlers, but most of them had strung out along the Pacific coast. "I suppose now that much of the best land has been taken up, the late-comers have to take their chances on the semi-arid land." He shuddered. "They've only heart-break ahead. There's not enough rainfall to grow grass enough on three hundred acres to feed one cow!"

The next morning Richardson came to him. "Major, I'm quitting. The ranchers will loan me a horse so I can ride out to the nearest settlement."

"Very well," he answered, secretly relieved.

On June 25 the expedition stopped at the mouth of the Yampa River for a week's scientific work. No matter how strenuous the day, after supper there was always a bit of singing. Fred Dellenbaugh proved expert on the mouth organ and played popular ditties the crew could sing.

On the morning of the Fourth of July, the Major wakened to the sound of gunfire. Alarmed, he leaped out of his blankets. Fred called out, "Nothing wrong, Major. I'm just celebrating Independence Day."

Powell scratched the sleep out of his eyes. "So it is!" he told the roused crew. "Well, boys, I think you've earned a day of rest."

They cheered. Andy had stowed away a jug of syrup for a special occasion, and served this with plate-sized flapjacks. Everyone lolled in camp, fished, and hunted. Everyone except the Major. His idea of a holiday was to keep working at top speed. That night Andy served thick ham slices, beans, corn bread, and tinned peaches. But there was one more surprise. Fred Dellenbaugh burrowed in his knapsack and produced a box of chocolates. They had melted and run together. "But they're chocolates!" the men crowed, polishing off the box in a few rounds.

Several evenings later the Major talked privately with Harry Thompson. He had marveled at the way the quiet professor had taken to mapmaking and worked smoothly as second-in-command. After he had expressed appreciation for Thompson's labors, he said, "Confidentially, I'm worried about Emma. Would you mind if I went ahead to the Uintah? I want to see if there's mail waiting for me at the Ute agency. I'm also looking for some word from Hamblin about that supply route down the Dirty Devil."

Thompson, more familiarly known as "the Prof," urged his brother-in-law to go ahead. He would see to everything.

"I'll take Walter with me to help bring back some supplies."

Wes' concern over Emma was not groundless. On arriving at the Indian agency, he found a letter waiting for him from Nellie to the effect that Emma was ill and needed him. There was bad news from Hamblin too. His letter said that he had not found the supply route. The Major groaned. "This means that the food you will take back to the river will have to last a lot longer than we anticipated."

Walter shrugged. "We've been having it good up to now. A few lean days won't hurt. You head out for Salt Lake. I'll get some Indians to tote this stuff to the river."

Torn between his scientific work and Emma's needing him, he reasoned rightly that Harry Thompson could carry on with Walter's help. "It will take some time for the crew to get this far if they do all the work I assigned them. Tell Harry that if Emma improves, I will be back at the mouth of the Uintah the twenty-sixth of July."

When Wes arrived in Salt Lake City after many hours in the

saddle, he found Emma much improved. Seeing him, if only briefly, made her feel even better, so he was able to leave shortly, and rejoined the men on schedule. But he did not continue downriver with them.

"I've got to find that route down the Dirty Devil, or we may find ourselves in dire straits," he confided to the dependable topographer. "I guess I'll have to go overland to Kanab, and try to locate the route myself. Can you carry on if I make out a work schedule?"

The Prof, who had managed smoothly during the Major's previous absence, nodded.

"Look for me at the Gunnison Crossing about September third."

While the Major was gone, the crew took three weeks poking through Desolation Canyon. They reached the Gunnison four days ahead of their leader. When he arrived with limited supplies of jerked beef, flour, and sugar, he, too, admitted failure to find the Dirty Devil route. "We have no choice," he was honest with his men. "We have to tighten our belts until we reach the Crossing of the Fathers."

The tenderfeet agreed. They had experienced little hardship and no hunger so far. Short rations could be endured, if only so they would have more daring tales to tell once they were home again.

The next two weeks the Powell Survey mapped, and had no trouble running Labyrinth and Stillwater canyons. On September 15 the junction of the Grand and the Green was reached. By this time food was a little too scant for comfort. A few grumbled and the Major ordered: "No more complaining out loud. If you must, confine your complaints to your diaries!" When they understood that he would tolerate no whining, he gave another order far less to their liking: "From here on our thrice-daily rations will consist of three strips of bacon and a chunk of bread for each man. We have plenty of coffee."

By the time the boats reached the Dirty Devil, the men were

in near-desperate straits. To save time the Major ordered the *Cañonita* cached, and hurried through the easy water of Glen Canyon.

"What about the mapping?" the Prof worried as mile after mile passed without time out for sketching.

"You and I could hold out," the Major told him, "but I've got to consider the others. We'll come back to this section after we've contacted the mule train."

Thanks to his careful advance planning, there was a packer and well-laden mule train waiting at the Crossing of the Fathers. Spirits revived after Andy served a whopping meal of ham, biscuits and gravy, beans, tinned tomatoes, and stewed dried prunes.

Once more the Major decided to leave the river. He had two reasons this time, only one of which he confided to Thompson. He was still worried about Emma. The other was simply that he had lost interest in the Colorado now that Harry Thompson could carry on the work. This second expedition had been routine. Whenever he found a meticulous person who would assume responsibility, the Major always delegated authority and moved on to another project.

While Powell journeyed to Salt Lake City, the reliable Prof went back to retrieve the *Cañonita,* mapped the missing portions, and then ran the leaky boats down to the mouth of the Paria. Here he cached them and led the men overland to Kanab, Utah, where he set them to constructing winter quarters.

By the time the Major and Emma and three-month-old baby Mary arrived in January, there were floored tents for his family, the Prof and Nelly, the crew, and a large tent containing drafting tables, file cases, and work tables. The two families were overjoyed at being reunited. They were also delighted with the thriving Mormon town and its homes, orchards, and gardens growing in irrigated soil. The women had company enough to keep them happy, and the geology roundabout fascinated the Major and Thompson.

One day in January the Prof mentioned regretfully, "We've accomplished an awful lot, Wes, but there is so much more that could be done if we had another year to work out here." By this time Thompson was thoroughly dedicated to mapping the canyon and plateau province, and hated to leave the job half finished.

Powell thought a bit. "If you can run the camp here, I'll go to Washington and try to wangle another appropriation to cover more field work."

"Then do it!" Thompson urged. "The sooner the better!"

The Major buzzed around Washington for months and finally secured the appropriation. Army experience and four wilderness expeditions had made him expert in getting his way. But he did more. Once he realized that Washington was fast becoming one of the world's great scientific centers, he severed his relations with Illinois Normal and decided to make the capitol his home.

Emma was thrilled. She persuaded him to buy a modest home in the 900 block on M Street Northwest. She furnished a study at the second floor rear. With walls lined with bookcases, there was still room for a drafting table, desk and chair. Evenings, after the baby was put to bed, Emma brought in her rocker and sewed and talked constantly. Wes so loved having her near him that he learned to shut his ears to her chatter and to work undisturbed.

His russet beard, maimed arm, and forceful stride soon became a familiar sight as he moved between his study and a small office in the red-towered Smithsonian. He was preparing a detailed report to accompany Thompson's maps, but just how he was now working for the Smithsonian, and not the Interior Department, was never explained.

On Sundays he relaxed with Emma and took his small toddling daughter, when she got a little older, to a nearby park. With fellow scientists, he played whist and bowled. When the city crowded him in, he drove a double team at a fast pace out into the country. Always his fertile mind was thinking, thinking. He did not intend to become a "city" man just yet. "There are still so many things to be done out West," he fumed over his unrealized studies. "The work of just one survey like mine is not enough. I've got to find some way of uniting all the surveys so they can concentrate on a Western program."

"What would you think of a unified survey?" he asked Professor Henry one day when they were cataloguing the Indian relics he had sent from the pueblos. "I mean, consolidate all government geological and topographical surveys as a United States Geological Survey, under one director, so there would be no wasted efforts or monies spent in duplication."

"Wonderful!" Professor Henry agreed enthusiastically. "But it will never come to pass! Too many personalities involved! Too much professional jealousy."

Meanwhile Harry Thompson grew a bit restless out in the canyon country. Since the Major had left him free to plan the field work for the second year of the survey, the stolid map-maker had taken the bit in his teeth. "Hamblin couldn't find a route from Kanab to the Dirty Devil," he mused one day while his wife worked beside him as his secretary. "Nor Wes. I think I'll move out there and have a look around."

The "look-around" was anything but casual. The Prof led his crew a breathless chase up and down valleys, around mesas and buttes, and discovered a little-known river whose mouth the Major had overlooked entirely in passing down the Colorado. Once he was sure this was not the Dirty Devil, the Prof followed it to its headwaters, mapped it, and called it the Escalante. Thus he assured himself of a small piece of fame by putting America's last-named river on a map.

Still not satisfied, he back-tracked and, after several failures, stumbled on a trail to the Dirty Devil. He followed it down to the Colorado, arriving on June 22, 1872. Here he divided his crew, sending some upriver to retrieve the *Cañonita* while he properly surveyed the river between the mouths of the Dirty

Devil and the Paria. As arranged previously, Powell met him there with provisions.

The Major resumed his position as leader. "All right, boys," he told his reassembled crew taking their places in the three boats, "now for the big one, the Grand Canyon!"

The going was rugged, but not nearly as desperate as the first trial. By September 8 the Major sighted the Virgin and called to the two boats behind the *Emma Dean II*, "Our voyage is done!" The news was received with three rousing cheers.

On the way back to Kanab, Utah, where the lengthy work of mapping the Colorado and the surrounding plateau province would be completed, Powell confided in his brother-in-law his plan to work toward the consolidation of the surveys.

Thompson understood. "You want to put the mapping job on my shoulders, so you can be off again to Washington. It's fine with me."

"It isn't that I don't want to stay with the mapping," Wes assured him. "It's just that I've got bigger fish to fry!"

CHAPTER EIGHTEEN

HELPING THE PAIUTES

Professor Henry was right about the idea of a consolidated survey not being acceptable because too much professional jealousy would be involved. Powell had to accept defeat, despite a vigorous campaign, but those closest to him knew he would keep on working quietly for an ultimate victory. Meanwhile he had his hands full.

From 1872 to 1877 he crammed every waking hour with a half-dozen interests. Summers he spent in the field with his survey, digging hard to unearth the full story of the plateau province: its geology, drainage, climate, resources, fossils, and Indians. He felt he was racing against time. As he had anticipated, westering Americans, finding less and less good land available, were moving into the arid region, courting disaster because they did not know how to operate in a dry-land area. The old tried-and-true farm methods were not applicable in the region of scant rainfall.

Eight months of each year the Major buzzed between his study and the Smithsonian, under whose sponsorship the reports of his plateau-province studies would be published. Whenever Emma pressed him, he wrote for magazines and newspapers and lectured. He was up to his ear in politics, getting continuing appropriations for his survey. He reveled in the association of other scientists and enjoyed good health. His thinking matured, and his prestige grew steadily.

During these years he was pulled two ways: by geology and by his intense interest in the Indian tribes of Western America. Gradually he dealt himself out of geology by delegating the field work to reliable Prof Thompson and other capable assistants. However, what he surrendered in geology, he gained in ethnology, his Indian studies.

Powell knew that the Indian was going to be dispossessed throughout America. "It's inevitable," he said regretfully. "That's why I feel an obligation to record their vocabularies and mythology, and collect their handwork before it is completely debased and altered by their contacts with the whites." Professor Henry lauded him for his devotion to the cause.

In 1872 he received a request from G. W. Ingalls, a newly appointed Indian agent. "Will you help some starving Paiutes find their place of survival in a world that wants only their total destruction?" the government man wrote him. When Ingalls had accepted the appointment as agent in southeastern Nevada, he found himself face to face with tragedy. The former Indian agent, a thoroughly corrupt man, had so cheated his charges that they were destitute. Ingalls had to do two things: provide immediate relief and incorporate a long-range rehabilitation program. "I'm willing, but I desperately need help and guidance," he appealed to the Major.

Powell hurried West, not with a sense of Christian obligation but with real zest for the job. "I'm going on an ethnological picnic," he told Emma as she packed his field kit. Now that Emma had a growing daughter and a house of her own, she was content to stay home.

Ingalls and Powell rode across the entire arid district, distributing rescue supplies. In October the chiefs came out of their remote retreats to powwow at Kanab.

Chuarruumpeak and others remembered Kapurats. "Help us," they appealed to their white friend.

The Major spoke to them through an interpreter and what he knew of their tongue, saying, "Your only chance of survival lies in adopting the white man's way of farming, of growing your own food."

The Paiutes said, "No good. Grass all gone. Water holes all gone. White mans take away." But after parleying among themselves, they told him, "If Kapurats say farming good, make full belly, we will try it. You get us land."

Much encouraged, Ingalls and Powell hurried to Washington. The Federal Commissioner of Indian Affairs temporized. Settlers in the canyon country were continually sending in hysterical demands for punitive military expeditions against the Indians. He suggested that first the two men visit all the Indians of eastern Nevada and Utah, report on actual conditions, take a census if possible, and then recommend in writing possible locations for reservations. "I might be able to do something," he said vaguely, quite sure the two men would forget about their appeal.

Instead they hurried back to Salt Lake City and outfitted for another field trip that lasted from July through November. On the long train ride returning East, Powell wrote a remarkable report. He revealed there were no more than 5,500 Indians in Utah, Nevada, parts of Arizona, Idaho, and California.

"Driven from the valleys and hunting grounds, scratching a bare subsistence from the hostile country, the various tribes, in bands of two hundred or less, are retreating into the hinterland. The government can ignore them, so in time all will perish, or it can establish them on reservations."

The Major wasn't surprised when his report was received with indifference. He knew that few people in Washington were interested in the Indians' survival. Western Congressmen still hued to the old cry, "The only good Indian is a dead Indian!" Corruption in Indian affairs reached to the highest levels of officialdom.

When Emma said impatiently, "Oh, Wes, why do you wear yourself out on a lost cause?" he answered, "What Christian can face his Maker without having championed some lost cause?"

Despite the earnestness of his and Ingalls' efforts, the Indians benefited little. The reservation sites that the Major recommended were too "good" to be wasted on savages, since they contained valuable water sites, grass, timber, and untapped mineral resources. Monopolistic timber and water companies and land-hungry settlers blasted out their objections, drowning the Major's hopes.

The Bureau of Indian Affairs compromised, if only to be free of the hornet tactics of Powell and Ingalls. They set aside the Moapa Reservation for six Paiute bands. The Major had to be content for the time being. He was especially happy when, a year later, Ingalls wrote enthusiastically about crops of wheat, corn, meal, and squash being produced. "The Paiutes are good farmers. With a little help they can be self-supporting." Ingalls went on to ask for tools, seed, teachers.

Although the Major pitched right in and worked hard, his efforts were of no avail. Ingalls' request was turned down by his superior officers.

It wasn't Powell's or Ingalls' fault. The blame could not be put on any one man or bureau. Ignorance, a wholesale neglect of Christian stewardship, greed, and the nation's sociological immaturity would continue these injustices to the American Indian far into the enlightened twentieth century.

CHAPTER NINETEEN

A ONE-MAN TARGET

The Major returned from his visit with Ingalls in time to secure still another appropriation for his Cinderella Survey. His thrifty soul winced at the waste and duplication in the Western studies, and the disgraceful wrangling between two of the other survey leaders, Lieutenant Wheeler and Dr. Hayden. Once again he tried to have Congress unify all topographical mapping under a combined United States Geological Survey, and once more he failed. As usual, disappointment left no mark on him because he was too busy with other projects.

In a letter written monthly by Emma for circulation among the family, she mentioned, "Wes has four projects under way: a report of the Colorado canyon expeditions and tributary explorations; a study of the geology of the Uintah mountains; an analysis and interpretation of the arid lands of the plateau province; and an encyclopedia of Indian languages. I still serve as his amanuensis at home, but he has a marvelous office secretary now, a young man named Stanley-Brown who has a good scientific background. Wes says he is a jewel!"

In 1875 the first of the projects was published: *The Exploration of the Colorado River of the West and Its Tributaries Explored in 1869, 1870, 1871 and 1872.* The breath-taking story was widely read. The Major gave full credit to all who assisted him and shared the spotlight with Harry Thompson.

The Prof was content. The great map of the Colorado was almost entirely his. He and the Major worked amicably and carried this relationship into family affairs. Always affectionate, Wes was glad to have Harry and Nell close by. His younger brother Bramwell was in Washington too, making a name for himself as a progressive administrator of District of Columbia schools. Martha Powell Davis and Mary Powell Wheeler, the two older sisters, came East frequently campaigning for women's suffrage. Martha's husband would be in Congress in the 1890's. Lida, married and living in Kansas, was visited on his cross-country trips, as was Juliet, famous as a teacher of folk songs. Since Mother and Father Powell were gone now, bachelor Walter made his home with Juliet or Nell.

A lively correspondence kept the Powell children in contact with one another. Whenever one was in financial difficulty, another came to the rescue. Wes chuckled, "At times it seems to me that all the spare money among the Powells is in transit from one to another." Although privately considered a little too "strong-minded" and "a talker," Emma was accepted wholeheartedly.

Soon the Major released for publication *The Geology of the Uinta Mountains.* A solid scientific work, critics hailed it as being "illustrated by one of the most beautiful maps ever included in a government publication." The Prof had drawn this one two.

The report created a stir among scientists because in it the Major "unravelled the mystery of the rocks" in a revolutionary theory since widely accepted.

At that time geologists believed in "catastrophism": namely, that mountains are formed by gigantic reoccuring upheavals. Powell discarded this theory when the rocks in the Grand Canyon area told him a different story. He interpreted the formation as one of massive "uplift." A great block of the earth's crust rose slowly, not catastrophically, *lifting with it the river* that already had been at work millions of years cutting its deep channel. As the earth rose in a block, the peaks, valleys, buttes, mesas, and canyons were cut away by rain, wind, snow, and ice. The river continued its channeling, maintaining the same elevation in the process. However, because its bed had been uplifted, it was grinding into older and older rocks until finally the igneous rock from the earth's very core was exposed.

Thus Powell subscribed to a new theory of *uplift and erosion and sedimentation*. Since then these geological processes have been incorporated into a new science, physiography, the study of the development of the features of the earth's surface, another of John Wesley Powell's contributions.

There were to be more.

The Major had no time to rest on his laurels. In the summer of 1877 he was drawn into a major dogfight. Dr. Hayden, head of one of the Western topographical surveys, was determined to control all geological studies sponsored by the government. He figured that two of his opponents were out of his way: Clarence King, having finished his survey, was now devoting all his energies to mining geology, and Lieutenant Wheeler was nicely pigeonholed in the War Department.

Powell was Hayden's target, and he decided to get rid of the Major by discrediting his survey and influencing Congress to grant him no further appropriations for field work.

The Major was puzzled. "I don't know what ails Hayden. I've been advocating a unified survey for years, without once seeking to be the director."

Emma sniffed. "Hayden is jealous. Your survey has accomplished more, with less money and fewer men, than his."

The future looked dismal for the Cinderella Survey because, as Powell insisted, "I will not indulge in vicious retaliatory tactics against Hayden. I'll let my accomplishments speak for me."

Hayden's hatred of Powell increased after the Major's third project was published. It was a small monograph entitled *A Report on the Lands of the Arid Region of the United States with a More Detailed Account of the Lands of Utah*. It contained much of his revolutionary thinking in the as-yet-unheard-of field of conservation.

In *Arid Lands*, the Major tried to help the small homesteader, second nature for a farm boy. He fought to shatter two wide-spread misconceptions. The first was that the area west of the 100th Meridian, west of the Dakotas, Kansas, Nebraska, Oklahoma, and Texas, was "the great American desert."

"This fourteen hundred mile strip of public domain, comprising two-fifths of the nation, is not," he insisted, "a forbidding wasteland of drifting sand." The Mormons had proved that the soil was very fertile when irrigated.

As Powell saw it, water was the key to opening the treasure chest of the plateau province.

The second misconception he attacked was more vicious; it was the popular belief that "rain follows the plow." The West was currently enjoying a wet cycle, or period of ample rainfall. It seemed that wherever men frontiered after the War, rains came to succor crops and pastureland. But the Major, through his studies, had discovered that in the past there had been intensive cycles of drought in this region. He knew there was disaster ahead for those who settled too far from a source of water.

One Sunday when Wes relaxed in his study for a talk with Bram, he said, "I know, but I can't convince others, that much of the arid lands, which the railroads and unscrupulous land companies are foisting onto gullible homesteaders, will never support man or animal without supplementary water." Unfortunately much of the river-bottom land was controlled by large livestock companies, and much of the water rights held by monopolistic companies who charged exorbitant rates for irrigation water. "The poor man is in for a licking," he foretold.

"Trying to help the poor man is a thankless job, Wes," Bram said.

His brother chuckled. "Don't I know it! But someone has to try to help the poor devils, even if it means taking a lot of abuse.

I don't mind being a one-man target. The railroads and land companies have already hired hacks to write scurrilous articles about me, and I couldn't care less! The only thing I do worry about is that they will strangle my survey. You know, of course, that many of the Western representatives in Congress are little more than puppets manipulated by the big-moneyed interests."

Bram nodded. "It's common knowledge."

Wes pointed out, "Lumber barons are making vast fortunes selling the timber that protects the watersheds whence the water issues. This is not timber on their privately owned lands, mind you. It's on federal domain, public land! They're getting away with downright thievery! And another thing, for hundreds of years the Indians have set forest fires to drive out wild game. So between them and the timber thieves, the future economic development of the region is imperiled, because it cannot produce without water."

He went on, unaware that he was making a startling prophecy concerning the future reclamation of the plateau province, "The government, because of the terrific cost, is going to have to build big dams and canals someday, to store and distribute the water out there. Of course, even I can see that much of the region will never offer more than spectacular scenery, and," he added drily, "you can't eat scenery."

Powell was thinking in terms of human welfare. He wanted to avert tragedy. He warned over and over, in publications and speeches, "The drought period is almost at hand." No one paid the slightest attention. It almost broke his heart when even the little people whom he was trying to help, and the Congressmen whom he was trying to enlighten, refused to act on the truths he laid before them.

He tried in vain to have Congress set up a land-use program geared to dry-land conditions. As a result, thousands of homesteaders were cheated and ruined, the land's resources pillaged, and the land itself abused. Many years would pass before his prophetic and crusading ideas would find acceptance. Not until 1908 would the idea of conservation be reborn in the fertile mind of Gifford Pinchot, founder of the United States Forest Service, and be drafted into a national conservation policy during President Theodore Roosevelt's administration.

Yet for the Major these were not dark days. Although he was fighting a losing battle on one front, he won on another. In March, 1879, Congress finally authorized the formation of a United States Geological Survey.

Immediately Washington buzzed with speculation. Rumor lent credence to the alleged war and struggle for power between Dr. Hayden and Major Powell. Everyone asked, "Who will get the directorship of the combined surveys?"

Hayden worked like a man possessed to get the appointment. He belittled Powell savagely and puffed up his own importance. He went too far. Congressmen became so disgusted with his antics that they refused to recognize his brazen bid for the directorship. Since Lieutenant Wheeler was also not popular, the final consideration narrowed to Clarence King and John Wesley Powell.

King was interviewed privately. "I don't want to take on the organization of a new bureau," he said frankly. "I have a good mining prospect in Mexico and I want to work there. What about Powell? He's your man."

The legislators discovered that the Major was not available! "I'm too busy with my Indian studies," he told them. He could not be wooed back to geological matters.

So the Congressmen decided, "If we can't have Powell, it has to be King." His name was presented to the House and confirmed by the Senate in April, 1879, largely because of Major Powell's insistence!

Powell was content. He told Professor Henry, "I know King will see that the work on the plateau-province studies will be continued."

Thus Clarence King became the first director of the United States Geological Survey. He accepted for the prestige and, frankly, to hamstring Dr. Hayden. He never planned to stay in office. "I'll do a minimum of organization," he confided to his closest associates, "and then ease friend Powell into the directorship a year from now."

CHAPTER TWENTY

"NO FROCK COAT FOR ME!"

The bill that created the United States Geological Survey also established the Bureau of Ethnology, and John Wesley Powell accepted the directorship with great pleasure and anticipation.

The evening of the day he assumed his new post, he burst through the front door of his Washington home, shouting, "Emma! Wait till you hear the good news!"

Emma hurried from the kitchen, her fingers floured with biscuit dough. "You look so excited, Wes. What happened?"

He held her tight, his one arm around her waist. "Congress finally saw the light! Remember that report I made last November to the Secretary of the Interior, practically begging him to set up a new bureau to tackle a thorough study of our Indians? It worked! Congress established a Bureau of Ethnology today! Think of it! After all these years, we're finally going to have an organization, and money for ethnological studies." He kissed his wife and then stepped back, gesturing excitedly. "No more haphazard poking around Indian mounds. No blind-alley studies. Ethnology is going to be organized as a *science,* and made a direct ally to help our Indians!" He turned and started up the stairs. "Come, I'll show you."

"I just put the biscuits in the oven."

"Hang the biscuits!" The Major took the stairs two at a time.

Emma hurried after him, rolling her hands in her apron. Hearing her parents' excited voices, eight-year-old Mary dropped the beetle she was mounting, and ran into the study. She saw her father hauling dozens of notebooks from his bookshelves. "What's the matter?"

"Look at these," the Major said. "One vocabulary after another. I've made hundreds of them, and they've had to gather dust for want of organization! Now we can start work on a real encyclopedia of Indian languages."

"How nice!" Emma exclaimed, happy for her husband.

"And that's only the beginning." He pulled folder after folder from the shelves. "Look at this monograph on the handcraft of the Paiute Indians. What good is it, buried on my shelf, or the Smithsonian's? That monograph could be a tool to help rehabilitate the Paiutes! You know what we're going to do? Give science a swift kick and make it come alive and help our Indians." He put his arm around Mary. "You see, before we can help our Indians, we have to know more about them. With the right kind of information shoved under its nose, the Bureau of Indian Affairs will have to do right by these poor people."

Emma was used to spinning in her husband's cyclonic enthusiasms. Mary clapped her hands. She didn't quite understand, but it must be wonderful if her father wanted to do it.

Wes raked his fingers through his hair, then paced the study. He figured that, properly administered, a Bureau of Ethnology could render a great service to the nation. It could enlist amateurs, students, and museum directors everywhere to take part in the studies. "Remind me to write anthropologists and paleontologists, and ask them to contribute," he told Emma, who nodded. She was still acting as his secretary at home.

"What good are collections and vocabularies unless their meaning and interrelations are interpreted?" he muttered, thinking out loud. There were dozens of federal activities dealing with the Indian at present, but not a single one coordinating with another. He clenched his fist. "There must be organization, and concentrated purpose . . ." He ticked off other goals, ideas spilling from him like cranberries from a basket.

Emma kept nodding enthusiastically, then suddenly she asked, "Who's going to supervise this new work?"

"I am!" Wes said offhandedly, without stopping his pacing.

"Are you going to work under Professor Henry at the Smithsonian?"

"No, no!" Her husband seemed a little nettled, as if she should know better. Then a new idea occurred to him, one that he had to get on paper at once. He dashed to the desk and began scribbling.

Emma asked impatiently, "Who is going to head this new Bureau of Ethnology?"

"I am," Wes answered. "Don't interrupt, Emma. I've got to work out this idea on paper."

Emma looked as if she had been struck by lightning. Her Wes, *Director* of the Bureau of Ethnology! "Well, why didn't you say so?" she exclaimed, flapping her apron. She was so exasperated. Honestly, what could you do with a man like that? He is appointed to an important government post and doesn't think that is worth telling! All he could see was the work not the prestige. Suddenly she remembered something. She shrieked, "The biscuits!"

Mary jumped and shrieked too.

The two rushed downstairs. Emma grabbed a potholder and yanked the pan out of the oven. "Oh, dear! They're ruined!"

Mary said, wide-eyed, "Golly, they're black all over."

For a moment Emma wanted to cry. Then her back straightened. Her Wes was only forty-five, and already a bureau director. She imagined him in an elegant new frock coat, receiving dignitaries in his office, giving orders to a roomful of clerks and stenographers, invited to the most elite social functions . . . Swiftly her mind set to figuring how the family budget could squeeze out enough for the frock coat for Wes, a new gown for her, maybe a new settee in the parlor. Maybe she could send

Mary to that fashionable dancing school. Maybe she could afford that tea set she had wanted for so long. There was much ado about calling cards and tea parties in Washingtons' social life, and Emma decided that it was time she had a part in it. Now that her Wes was an important man, she must help him meet the right people.

"Come, help Mother fix another batch of biscuits," she told Mary. She was smiling. Maybe she and Wes wouldn't be climbing mountains together on this new job, but there were other things to share. "Your daddy is a very important man now," she impressed on Mary. "He is a bureau director. We will have to get him an elegant black frock coat."

"Will you get him a new hat too?" Mary asked, giggling. She knew how her Mother fussed over the Major's dilapidated old hat.

When Emma broached the subject of the frock coat to Wes, he gasped. "A frock coat! Emma! Don't you know me better than that! I won't wear one! I won't have time for social functions. I am going to make the Bureau of Ethnology one of the best-functioning scientific bureaus in Washington, and I simply will not be bothered with such nonsensical trappings. I suppose the next thing you will suggest is a tall silk hat!"

Emma sighed. She knew there was no use nagging. Wes would not wear the frock coat.

Neither did he wall himself behind clerks and secretaries. His office was off the bureau's main room, the door always open. He would not further his social position by attending elite parties. As always, his associates were fellow scientists who bothered none about fashionable talk. Powell lived science, talked science, breathed science, with time out for an occasional cigar or glass of wine, and a walk to the park or nearby Rock Creek Gorge with Mary. There he introduced his daughter to nature's wonderful story, just as George Crookham had done for him when he was her age.

"The only social affairs I want are getting together with my sisters and brothers," he told Emma, who had to give up her dreams of being prominent in society. Instead, she hauled her little rocker and basket of mending into the study, and talked a steady stream while her husband shut his ears and pursued his vast new program. Mary had her rocker there too, and burrowed in a book, ignoring everything but the exciting story on the printed pages.

In one year, by enlisting the help of amateurs, specialists, and collaborators all over the country, John Wesley Powell brought to ethnology a scope and usefulness and purpose never dreamed possible. Thus he served the American Indian as no other man had in the past or would in the future. However much Powell recognized the worth of scientific study, he geared those studies to the higher purpose of helping the Indian.

George Crookham, now dead, would have been proud of his pupil.

CHAPTER TWENTY-ONE

DIRECTOR OF THE UNITED STATES GEOLOGICAL SURVEY, 1881-1894

Time passed too quickly for the Major as he labored to expand the scope of the infant Bureau of Ethnology. He was surprised one morning to receive a call from the White House. "Major Powell? Stanley-Brown," the young man identified himself. "How are you, sir?"

"Fine!" was the exuberant answer. "How is your new job?"

An expert at shorthand and typing, Stanley-Brown had served as the Major's valued secretary for several years. When a mutual friend of theirs, James A. Garfield, was elected president of the United States in 1880, the Major gave up Stanley-Brown so that he could become private secretary to the new executive. "The job is wonderful. But that's not what I called about. Would you have time for a quiet chat with the President this afternoon?"

The Major's ears buzzed. A quiet chat, eh? he thought. He knew better. "What's up?" he asked.

Stanley-Brown evaded the question, saying, "About two, Major?"

Powell agreed and hung up. Several hours later he was ushered into the President's office. Garfield greeted him like an old friend and pointed to a suave man. "You and Clarence King need no introduction."

King and Powell shook hands. Each had a high regard for the other's accomplishments as geological survey directors. When they were seated, President Garfield said, "King, suppose you break the news."

"Major Powell, I was made the first director of the United States Geological Survey, largely as a result of your recommendation. I believe I have expressed my gratitude to you, both in private and publicly."

"Your reputation assured you the directorship, sir."

King continued. "I am resigning the directorship. I didn't want the job in the first place. To be perfectly honest, I haven't done much with it. However, before I handed in my resignation, I talked with friend Garfield here, to make sure he would put the best-qualified man in America in that job." His eyes lighting with pleasure, King exclaimed, "I have his promise that you will succeed me as Director."

The Major was stunned for a moment. When he assumed the directorship of the Bureau of Ethnology, he thought he had turned his back forever on geology. "I'm overwhelmed," he admitted, "but what about my Indian studies? I —— "

Garfield and King laughed. "Surely a man of your energy could run two bureaus," the President complimented Powell.

"Two bureaus! Then I wouldn't have to give up ethnology!" Wes felt his heart pounding, the way it had that moment he had topped Long's Peak and viewed the vast province of the Colorado spread out below. "In that case, I accept!"

Stanley-Brown tossed decorum to the winds. "Hooray! At last!"

The quiet talk bubbled with good wishes until President Garfield brought a more serious tone to the conversation. "Major

Powell, as Director of Geological Survey, I charge you with two major responsibilities: a classification of the public land into such proper categories as arable land, irrigable land, desert, timber, and mineral land. Most of this lies west of the one hundredth meridian, as you well know. This land must be classified so the people moving Westward will know what conditions they must face. Second, I charge you with an examination of the mineral resources of the public domain. As soon as the Senate confirms your nomination, I hope you will start action at once."

"I will, sir!" The first duty appealed to him strongly. He thought, "Now I'll get in some official licks for the poor man's benefit."

Knowing that the President always faced a heavy schedule of appointments, Clarence King rose. Once more he shook hands with Powell and complimented him. "Thanks to you, Major, we have a United States Geological Survey. Now I look forward to what that Survey is going to accomplish under your directorship. Good luck, and God bless your work!"

"We'll expect great things of you," Garfield added warmly.

"I won't fail you," the Major assured them as Stanley-Brown escorted him out of the President's office. There the secretary wrung his hand. "Go to it, sir. It's taken a long time, but now you have a clear track ahead."

As he hurried to his own office, the Major realized why Stanley-Brown had invited him for a "quiet" chat. Dr. Hayden had spies everywhere reporting on Powell's activities, and would have moved mountains to keep him from getting the directorship. Wes knew that Hayden's rage would be terrible when he learned that he had been by-passed. He felt genuinely sorry for the man. Not for one moment did he take any pleasure in having been chosen over Hayden, whose promising career was destined to disintegrate because of his lamentable lack of character.

The Major decided not to tell Emma the good news until after the Senate confirmation.

Once he got used to running two bureaus, he saw beyond the immediate and obvious work to the vast potentialities. Just as being atop Long's Peak revealed the Colorado to him, and mapping the Colorado unfolded the plateau province to him, so now his dual directorship enabled him to enlarge the horizons of government-sponsored science.

Night after night he worked in his study, mapping in his mind and on paper how the Geological Survey could best serve both mankind and science.

Emma, aware only that he was unusually preoccupied, said, "Some new project under way, Wes?" Mary, reading as usual, raised her head.

He nodded.

The rocker squeaked a while, then Emma asked, "Having trouble with the encyclopedia?"

It was some time before he answered, "No."

Since she couldn't bear to be left uninformed, Emma persisted. "A new job, darling?"

"Mmmmhunh," he mumbled, his fingers knotted in his graying hair.

When he said nothing more, Emma, just a shade exasperated, said, "Well, what is the new job?"

No answer.

After a while Wes spun around and shot a question at her. "Emma, can you see any reason why geology has to be confined to the popular notion that it is something to do with rocks? Couldn't geology include all sorts of related subjects, such as paleontology and topographical mapping and surveying and botany and ——" He paused, then rushed on. "As I see it, a geological survey could be one of the greatest fact-finding agencies in the world. It could include studies of rocks, rivers, fossils, insects, minerals, deserts, forests, flood control, irrigation, watersheds" — he took a breath — "and include mineralogy, stratigraphy, geophysics, everything that has anything to do with man, the ground he walks on and cultivates, and the earth beneath!"

"Oh, Wes," Emma said in her positive way, "no one survey could encompass all that! Take just one thing you mentioned, topographical mapping. You know it takes ages to do a good map of just one small area, by the time you include every road, town, bridge, lake, river, every hundred-foot variation in elevation. Why, there's a lifetime of work in mapping, let alone a geological survey or any of those others you mentioned. Good heavens, no man could keep all those lines of investigations going without their becoming hopelessly snarled."

Mary spoke up brightly. "Daddy could."

"That's my girl!" the Major smiled at her. Then he turned back to his desk and studied the inked sheets. Before the Civil War, government scientific activities had been the concern of the Smithsonian Institution; the states dabbled in geology; Army Engineers took care of mapping; the Navy looked into "climatology," the weather. Powell wanted all scientific work brought under one Department of Science. A good place to start was in the United States Geological Survey, the outgrowth of his own Cinderella Survey.

Emma had resumed her rocking, but paused when she heard him mutter, "You're wrong. I know I could keep my finger on all that, and ethnology too."

His wife eyed him affectionately. Her great man must not be discouraged, not even in his wildest daydreaming! Still, she felt free as usual to air her opinion. "Darling, how would one man ever have the opportunity to do all that? What you're suggesting is centralizing all federal scientific studies under one head. That's too big, too ambitious! No one bureau could handle it."

"The U.S.G.S. could," he answered, using the popular way of referring to the United States Geological Survey.

"Is that one of Clarence King's grandiose schemes?" she asked a trifle scornfully.

"No. Mine."

"But you don't have anything to do with the U.S.G.S.!" she pointed out, drawing heavily on her patience.

"Do too," he answered. "I'm the new director." Then he withdrew into the complex world of his creative thinking and would say nothing more.

Emma sputtered. She gasped, rocked furiously a moment, stopped. "Did I hear right?" she asked Mary.

Mary looked up from her book. "He's the new director," she said and returned to her story. She was used to a papa who was forever being named director of something.

Emma half rose, meaning to hug Wes, but sank back and started rocking slowly. There were times when even she couldn't keep up with John Wesley Powell.

Once confirmed in his new position, Major Powell made good his promise to President Garfield. Within weeks he had crews in the field on the land-classification project. Others tackled the minerals survey, topographic mapping, an irrigation survey, a hundred separate projects, all valuable to man's knowledge of how to live well on the land.

Year after year, with constantly increased appropriations, hundreds of full-time and part-time workers, research collaborators, and student assistants, Major Powell expanded the U.S.G.S. until it worked in fields far beyond the scope of "rocks," just as he had planned that night in his study.

Undeniably his pet project was enormous, enough to absorb all the waking hours of any bureau. Powell outlined and began systematic work on the long-needed task of assembling a complete, detailed topographical atlas of the United States. "That way everyone — farmer, stockman, mining man, Congressman, businessman, government employee, scientist, or student — will know the exact location and elevation and terrain of every inch of the United States," he explained in a newspaper interview.

It was a monumental task. "I figure it will take twenty years and eighteen million dollars to complete."

He was wrong. Sixty years have passed since then, the work is not yet 50 per cent completed, and the cost is now over 100,000,000 dollars!

Another major accomplishment of those early years as Director was his idea to standardize a system of nomenclature, diagrams, and mapping symbols that found world-wide acceptance, thus ending the confusion that existed in geological, geographical, and mapping studies up to that date.

The geological studies he relegated to Professor Thompson, Grove Karl Gilbert, and Captain Clarence E. Dutton. Thompson finished mapping the Green and White Rivers, the Colorado and Paria, and much of the plateau province.

Gilbert, a much-loved man, systematized *The Geology of the Henry Mountains*, a range that Powell named for Professor Henry of the Smithsonian. Once Gilbert was in the field, he was told to stay as long as he wished and develop his own lines of inquiry. The freedom and trust, and opportunity to have his work published as Survey documents, gave him a chance to develop into a great scientist.

As for Captain Dutton, he was interested in land forms and erosion. He did yeoman work on *The Physical Features of the Valley of the Colorado*. His lasting claim to fame came with the publication of *A Tertiary History of the Grand Canyon District*, which contained some of the most colorful "verbal landscape painting" ever published in a scientific monograph. Illustrated by the boldly spectacular paintings of Thomas Moran, and the startling line drawings of William Henry Holmes, this volume on the Grand Canyon is now considered one of the most beautiful books ever published on our country's Western explorations.

Powell also brought into the Survey one of the great paleontologists of his day, Othniel C. Marsh, and gave him free rein to pursue research in his study of the ancient life of the globe, its fossil animal and plant organisms.

Next he incorporated studies of soil and grass as an aide to agriculture.

He established a division of mining statistics, investigated the country's mineral resources on public lands, and the most efficient methods of mining and processing ores.

The Major went still further. Although "my main objective was making science serve man," he said later that he saw a new and larger purpose in these studies. "The information being gathered must not only bring into clear focus unknown facts. It must show the way to conserve these resources for the future benefit of both the nation and its people."

Many historians now consider that the early history of the United States Geological Survey, under John Wesley Powell, is *the history of the beginnings of the conservation movement* in America.

"A group of us are chartering a National Geographic Society," a friend told him. "Would you have time to help us get it on its feet?"

He would.

"We need a Geological Society of America which all geologists can join for enlightenment and sociability, and help prepare papers to be read before the National Academy of Science," he decided one day. Gathering a few cronies among the geologists in Washington, he helped found the now well-known "G.S.A."

But the pace was beginning to show. At times he was nervous and irritable. His eyesight was impaired by an infection so that he had to use both a reader and an amanuensis. Even a leisurely trip to the pueblos with his brother Bram could not restore him to his usual enthusiastic, energetic self.

Year after year his department budget mushroomed. He alone

had control of the disbursement of hundreds of thousands of dollars. He hired and fired a small army of men. "There is no room for incompetents in the Survey," was the word passed around. His Survey had grown to a federal department of science.

Honors were heaped on him, professional degrees granted by colleges for his achievements, and honorary degrees as well. These meant little to the man who had never had the money to finish college. He received his honors modestly and promptly forgot them.

"My work is an obligation to mankind. I consider it a privilege to be a servant of the people," he said. He was not interested in fame or political power, though he had both in full measure.

Night and day he wrestled with science, making it serve America. He was too busy to pay any attention to the criticism that was slowly gathering over the years.

"He's sure getting cranky," more than one of his assistants admitted in time. No wonder! He had a thousand threads to keep straight. The constant burden of politics to keep the appropriations coming year after year wore him down. The stump of his arm began to bother him until he was never free from pain. The only periods of relaxation were those he enjoyed when his brothers and sisters and their children came to the house Sunday nights for supper and a songfest.

Then he ran into real trouble.

He further infuriated the big-moneyed interests of the West, the men who were making fortunes stealing or exploiting the public grasslands, water, timber, and minerals. "I hate them!" he thundered in the privacy of his office. "I'm going to do everything I can to stop them from ruining this country!" He advocated conservation measures and fought for a new program of federally built dams and irrigation projects that would give the poor man a fair share of the water.

He drew the fire of the exploiters. They blasted him in the newspapers and circulated vicious rumors about his being "power-mad," and "dictating to Congress."

As usual Powell would not retaliate. "I'm too busy to waste my energies on a dogfight. The accomplishments of my directorship speak for me. That's enough."

Tragically, it was *not* enough. The campaign of slander won out. Congress was pressured into stripping the United States Geological Survey of its huge appropriations. Worse, its future activities were confined largely to making the topographical atlas.

In one congressional stroke, Powell's tower of science crashed.

The shock almost broke his heart. "Not for myself. For America," he mourned.

He could not see that it was only a temporary setback. Fortunately he lived just long enough to know that, out of the seeds of his revolutionary thinking, and by the will of the long-suffering people, the government was forced to re-enter the field of conservation in order to save from utter destruction what was left of the country's natural resources. And out of Powell's thinking was to come eventually a mature and expanded Geological Survey, the United States Forest Service, Fish and Wildlife Service, Bureau of Mines, National Park Service, Reclamation Service, Soil Conservation Service, public dams, and irrigation projects.

And as always, John Wesley Powell faced the facts honestly and dispassionately. "I wanted too much for America," he said wearily. He had grown too big. Too many small, jealous men were eating away at his program. "It's time I retired."

On May 4, 1894, he resigned as Director of the United States Geological Survey. His only consolation was that his successor was one of the younger men who had explored the plateau province with him, brilliant, levelheaded Charles Walcott.

"Thank God I still have the Bureau of Ethnology," he said,

and turned his tremendous energies, however lessened they were by illness and age, to his Indian studies. He remained its Director until his death.

But the man who had conquered Long's Peak and the Colorado had to face the bitter truth. "I have outlived my usefulness."

CHAPTER TWENTY-TWO

GOOD-BY

"How does your husband like being retired?" friends asked Emma some time later.

"What retirement?" she would bridle. "The Major is busier than ever!"

The following seven winters the Major was up to his ears in scientific writing, lecturing, and administering his Bureau of Ethnology. He kept his office at the bureau and worked closely there with William J. McGee, a young genius whom he was grooming as his successor. McGee was a giant of a fellow, self-taught, possessed of the same indefatigable energy and creative mind as Powell. The two became inseparable. McGee was a frequent guest in the Powell home, particularly when the Major held open house several nights weekly.

One evening the Major and McGee were discussing the relationship between the size of a man's brain and his intelligence. They bandied arguments back and forth. "You know, I'll wager my brain is bigger than yours," the Major said.

McGee chortled. "No such thing! I'm bigger than you, so my brain is bound to be bigger than yours."

They swapped friendly insults until the Major said, "I'm serious, McGee. This is one argument I want settled. Why don't we agree that, after we die, our brains are to be removed and

179

weighed and measured by a specialist? We won't live to know the final results, but I'll wager mine is the larger."

McGee thought it was an excellent idea.

Emma was horrified. "How gruesome!"

"Not at all," the Major and McGee assured her.

The summers following his retirement were spent at "The Haven," a vacation resort near the town of Brookline on the Maine coast. The Powell cottage sat back among the pine trees, the front porch facing Central Harbor.

Emma was a very staid matron now, opinionated as ever, concerned with women's affairs and neighboring with other resort families. She no longer served as his amanuensis, having been replaced by quiet, capable May Clark, who was accepted as one of the family. Mary, vacationing from school, and later from teaching, devoted her summers to being a companion to both her parents.

In good weather the Major rose with the sun, slipped on a bathing suit, and waded out in the bay for a morning dip. After breakfast and a period of dictating to May Clark, he donned a Norfolk jacket, knickerbockers, wool stockings, and a soft fedora hat. Gripping a knobby spruce cane, he headed out for a walk along the shore. The wear and tear of years had changed him. He no longer bothered to stand tall; his waistline had thickened from too many years of sitting at a desk. His beard was stained with tobacco juice. But his gray eyes sparkled with the joy of living.

Children adored him and tagged after him, begging for songs, and especially for stories about the Indians out West.

The man who had run the Colorado could not stay away from boats. Before long he found a Yankee captain to guide him through the many bays and harbors of the north coastline.

One day, out on the water, he spotted a shell mound. "Take us ashore."

The Captain turned in and waited while the Major and his young friends dug happily for Indian artifacts. When they unearthed an arrowhead or fragment of pottery, he took time to tell the story of the tribesman who had dropped it there. When that midden, or shell heap, was riddled, he led his happy crew back to the boat and searched for another. Thus over the years the Major and his junior army explored much of the Maine coast. It was the highlight of the summer for many growing boys who never knew that Major Powell was trying, in his way, to repay a debt of gratitude for the wondrous things George Crookham had brought into his life.

The shoreline did not consume all his attention. Another day the boys wanted him to take them through the woodlands. "Shall we ride horses or walk?"

A small boy piped up. "You gotta ride a bicycle."

"A bicycle, eh?" the Major pondered. "Well, that might be a little risky for a man over sixty, but no one can ever say I backed away from a new experience."

An older boy said, "I'll loan you my two-wheeler."

When it was rolled before him, the Major forked the seat, grabbed the handle-bars, and pushed off with both feet. The bicycle turned in knots as he scrambled to keep his feet on the pedals. He ended up in the dust. His giggling companions picked him up.

"We'll try it again," he said gamely. "Confounded contraption!" he swore privately at the bicycle. The second try was also disastrous. This time he sat in the dust to think things over. Long's Peak hadn't stopped him, nor the Colorado. There must be some way of besting this infernal machine.

"Whyn't cha hire Ownie MacDonald to run behind you with one hand on the seat, so you won't go crooked?" one of the lads suggested. Ownie was a young hired hand who did odd jobs around the resort.

"Get him," the Major capitulated. With Ownie's help he had no more spills. The happy, noisy crew peddled merrily over many a country road after that.

Some time after this, in the winter of 1900-1901, the Major

decided, "We're going to Cuba. I want to putter around the prehistoric Indian ruins there."

Emma and Mary insisted that the trip would be too strenuous for him.

"Posh!" he ridiculed their fears. "I never had time to study the Arawak and Carib Indians. I mean to do it now."

Emma, Mary, May, and the Major trooped south. For a while Powell buzzed around the islands, more like his old self. But the heat and island fever laid him low. He was ill for weeks and returned north in a weakened condition.

The following winter he suffered a stroke and was confined to his bed for weeks. All the old-timers came to see him: Walcott, Gilbert, Thompson, and his sister Martha's brilliant son, Arthur Davis, who was making a name for himself as a topographer. McGee came every day.

One of the most encouraging things he learned was that President Theodore Roosevelt had declared: "It is as right for the National Government to make the streams and rivers of the arid region useful by engineering works for water storage as to make useful the rivers and harbors of the humid region by engineering works of another kind."

The Major smiled when Arthur Davis read this to him. "Well, well, well. The future is finally catching up with my ideas . . . These things take time." He told the young man, "You must learn to control impatience." Then he roared, "But always be impatient!"

By January, 1902, the Major was out of bed and ranting to go outside. Emma and the doctor refused but were worn down by his nagging. Tolly Spriggs, a Negro messenger from the bureau, offered to walk the Major to his office. "I'll see he don' skedaddle too fast," he promised.

They started out, the Major like a fire horse for a few steps. But his gait was shaky, and he puffed. "Come on! Faster!" he tugged on Tolly's sleeve. "I'm used to climbing mountains."

"You're doin' fine," Tolly fibbed as he guided the tottering man.

The men at the bureau were shocked at the Major's appearance. He was only sixty-eight, but looked a hundred. They humored him, moved his books nearer his desk, knowing he would do no more than shuffle a few papers around. Pretty soon he said, "Tolly, call a carriage and take me home."

It was his last trip to the bureau.

Most of the winter and spring he was ailing. In May he started pressing Emma to take him to Maine. On May 27, 1902, the family boarded *The Priscilla*, a coastal steamer they had traveled on for years. As they sailed past the Statue of Liberty, the Major squinted at it and said to Mary in a weak voice, "That wasn't there when your Grandpa and Grandma Powell came to America."

The trip exhausted him. "Aaaaah," he sighed with relief as he relaxed on the cottage porch, swathed in blankets. "The sun up north never gets as hot as it did that time in the canyon," he reminisced.

May Clark readied his study and called from the door, "Will you be doing any dictating this afternoon, Major?"

He was a long time answering. "N-no, let's wait until tomorrow."

Tomorrow came, and others, but the Major could not seem to put his mind to any one piece of work. He had severe pains in his chest and, as always, diagnosed his failing with complete honesty. "It's heart trouble. I know my days are numbered," he told himself.

On June 17 he heard more wonderful news. President Theodore Roosevelt had established a Reclamation Bureau. The arid region was to be reclaimed with dams and irrigation projects. A bright new era was beginning.

"What did I tell you?" he told Emma gleefully. "For twenty-five years I tried to make Congress see the need for it. Roosevelt and Pinchot and our boy McGee are going great guns on conservation." Then he added wryly, "I guess it took younger men to put it over."

His joy was even greater when he learned that his enterprising young nephew, Arthur Davis, was named assistant chief engineer of the Reclamation Bureau. "There's a Powell to carry on," he gloated.

On September 17, 1902, a gold and blue autumn day, Major Powell slipped into a coma from which he never recovered. By September 20 he was gone.

The old gang from the Cinderella Survey joined the family for the funeral services held in the parlor of the Washington home. He was laid to rest in Arlington National Cemetery. The active and honorary pallbearers included most of the outstanding scientists of his day.

The legacy left to Emma and Mary was modest: the house on M Street, his library, a small insurance policy, a few dollars in the bank, the memory of a devoted husband and father.

The legacy left to America was monumental: a United States Geological Survey, a Bureau of Ethnology, and a Reclamation Service. His vision of harnessing the mighty Colorado came to fruition with the construction of Hoover Dam in the Boulder project. He had brought into clear focus a great portion of his beloved country, the plateau province.

But how many tourists who view the Grand Canyon today and glance at the granite memorial to John Wesley Powell and the conquerors of the Colorado River appreciate the wonderful heritage this slight red-haired, one-armed man bequeathed to his country?

Not that the Major would care whether they did or not. He had the last laugh. When McGee died later, and a specialist weighed and measured the brains of the two friends, the Major proved to have the bigger, heavier brain.

What was more important, he had used it well!

BIBLIOGRAPHY

Bailey, Paul. *Jacob Hamblin: Buckskin Apostle.* Los Angeles, California, Westernlore, 1948.

Bowles, Samuel. *Across the Continent: A Summer's Journey to the Rocky Mountains, Mormons, and the Pacific States, with Speaker Colfax.* Springfield, Massachusetts, The Springfield Republican, 1866.

Corle, Edwin. *Listen, Bright Angel.* New York, Duell, Sloan & Pearce, Inc., 1946.

Darrah, William Culp. *Powell of the Colorado.* Princeton, New Jersey, Princeton University Press, 1951.

Dellenbaugh, Frederick. *A Canyon Voyage.* New York, G. P. Putnam's Sons, 1908.

Dutton, Clarence Edward. *A Tertiary History of the Grand Canyon District.* Washington, D.C., United States Geological Survey, 1882.

Fenton, Carroll Lane. *The Story of the Great Geologists.* New York, Doubleday, Doran & Co., 1945.

Foster-Harris. *The Look of the Old West.* New York, The Viking Press, Inc., 1955.

Freeman, Lewis. *The Colorado River.* New York, Dodd, Mead & Co., 1923.

Geological Society of America. *Fiftieth Anniversary Volume, 1888-1938.* New York, The Society, 1941.

Hibbard, Benjamin Horace. *A History of the Public Land Policies.* New York, The Macmillan Co., 1924.

King, Clarence. *First Annual Report of the United States Geological Survey.* Washington, D.C., Government Printing Office, 1880.

Miller, William. *An Introduction to Historical Geology.* New York, D. Van Nostrand Co., Inc., 1937.

Peattie, Donald Culross. *A Natural History of Western Trees.* Boston, Houghton Mifflin Co., 1950.

Pinchot, Gifford. *Breaking New Ground.* New York, Harcourt, Brace & Co., 1947.

Powell, John Wesley. *The Exploration of the Colorado River of the West and Its Tributaries Explored in 1869, 1870, 1871 and 1872.* Washington, Government Printing Office, 1875.

Robbins, Roy Marvin. *Our Landed Heritage: The Public Domain 1776-1936.* Princeton, New Jersey, Princeton University Press, 1942.

Schuchert, Charles, and Dunbar, Carl. *Textbook of Geology.* New York, John Wiley & Sons, Inc., 1929.

Stegner, Wallace. *Beyond the Hundredth Meridian.* Boston, Houghton Mifflin Co., 1953.

Taft, Robert. *Artists and Illustrators of the Old West.* New York, Charles Scribner's Sons, 1953.

———. *Photography and the American Scene.* New York, Charles Scribner's Sons, 1942.

Teale, Edwin Way. *Autumn Across America.* New York, Dodd, Mead & Co., 1956.

Waters, Frank. *The Colorado.* New York, Rinehart & Company, 1946.

INDEX